Brecon Beacons
40 favourite hill walks

The author and publisher have made every effort to ensure that the information in this publication is accurate, and accept no responsibility whatsoever for any loss, injury or inconvenience experienced by any person or persons whilst using this book.

published by
pocket mountains ltd
The Old Church, Annanside,
Moffat, Dumfries and Galloway DG10 9HB

ISBN: 978-1-907025-914

Text and photography copyright © Ben Giles 2023
First published 2010, this edition (with updates) published 2023

The right of Ben Giles to be identified as the Author of this work has been asserted by him in accordance with the Copyright, Designs and Patents Act 1988

A catalogue record for this book is available from the British Library

Contains Ordnance Survey data © Crown copyright and database 2023 supported by out of copyright mapping 1945-1961

All rights reserved. No part of this publication may be reproduced, stored in a retrieval system, or transmitted in any form or by any means, electronic or mechanical, including photocopying and recording, unless expressly permitted by Pocket Mountains Ltd.

Printed by J Thomson Colour Printers, Glasgow

Introduction

Since 1957, the Brecon Beacons have been designated a national park covering an area of more than 1300 sq km. From the long finger-like ridges of the Black Mountains and the border with the English county of Herefordshire in the east to the open and remote moorland uplands of Fforest Fawr and the county of Carmarthenshire in the west, from the iconic central peaks and steep escarpment of Pen y Fan towering above the town of Brecon to the reservoirs and headwaters of rivers that flow southwards to former mining valleys and towns, the Brecon Beacons provide some of the most varied hillwalking in Britain.

The area is surrounded by the market towns of Brecon, Llandovery and Hay-on-Wye to the north and to the south by Abergavenny and former mining centres, including Blaenavon and the one-time 'iron capital' of Merthyr Tydfil. Criss-crossing the hills are the former routes used by people since Neolithic times – the Romans built a network of roads linking their forts, and for centuries drovers from the west of Wales used the high routes to drive their stock to market.

The geology of the area is dominated by the underlying presence of old red sandstone, exposed strikingly in the steep north facing scarp slopes while, in the south, outcroppings of limestone give way to a landscape of sinkholes and underground cave systems. Millstone grit, too, can be seen – to miners' minds the 'farewell rock' marking the limit of the coal measures, but to modern eyes the cause of delightful cascades and waterfalls. The mighty rivers of South Wales – the Usk, Tawe, Neath and Taff – rise here too, their headwaters dammed to feed the working populations in the valleys below, at times plunging through steep-sided gorges, whose natural channelling has been exploited to power the industrial workings and machinery of past centuries. Now, however, the area is strictly managed, but by walking it is still possible to appreciate the history and landscape for oneself.

About this guide

This guide contains 40 circular routes, the majority of which are within the boundaries of the Brecon Beacons National Park. This collection of walks is split into five areas: the Black Mountains; the Llangattock and Llangynidr Hills; the Central Beacons; Fforest Fawr; and the Black Mountain (Y Mynydd Du). In part, the areas reflect the natural dividing lines of valleys and settlements, as well as the landscape's geology and ecology. However, the areas are in no way wholly distinct or separate, though each has its own particular attractions and character and in general there is a feeling of greater remoteness in the western part of the park.

Many of the routes visit the high tops and peaks, both those that are well known and a good number which are far less frequented. A number of lower-level routes have also been included for those wishing to explore the valleys, gorges and sites of past industry or as alternatives when the weather rules out the summits.

The length of the routes varies from less than a half day's stroll to a full day in the hills, while some routes could easily be combined to give longer outings. Each route includes information on time, height gained, distance and the recommended Ordnance Survey (OS) 1:25,000 map (for all routes, either OS Explorer OL12 or OL13). The time is based on an average walking speed of 4km per hour, with variations for terrain and height built in, and indicates the actual time needed for walking the route.

In addition, rests and stops, weather and seasonal conditions, and personal fitness and stamina will need to be taken into account. The route map is intended only as a general schematic guide and does not replace the need for navigation with an appropriate map and, at times, a compass.

Getting around

Most people who visit the Brecon Beacons come by car and the national park is well supplied with designated parking areas. The availability of public transport to the start locations of many of the walks is a real challenge. However, where it has been possible to start a walk from a town or village on a bus route, this has been taken into consideration. For bus routes and timetables visit www.traveline.cymru. If planning to arrive by train, there are stations on the edge of the national park at Abergavenny, Merthyr Tydfil, Llandovery and Llandeilo.

Cycling is popular and there are a number of marked trails, including the long-distance Taff Trail, all of which could be used to reach the start of routes. However, access by car is the preferred option for many and, where parking is outwith designated car parks, consideration should be shown to the needs and access of local residents.

Safety and access

On a balmy summer's day the hills of the Brecon Beacons offer seemingly limitless easy walking. None of the peaks are particularly high, many of the paths are worn clear through their popularity and only a minority of the routes in this guide are what could be called remote or over pathless terrain.

For these reasons it would be easy to assume that the usual conventions of proper equipment, fitness and navigation skills are not as vital in these hills as in other more remote ranges of the British Isles. However, self-reliance is essential for the enjoyment of these hills as for any other upland area.

Bad weather and very limited visibility occur frequently and quickly, at times requiring skilled use of map and compass. As a measure of this, it is worth noting that the Brecon Beacons is one of the areas that the military considers well-suited to training troops in proficiency in the outdoors.

The Countryside and Rights of Way Act 2000, which introduced a new right of access on foot to mapped open country and registered common land in England and Wales, has had a significant impact on the Brecon Beacons. In particular, it has opened up legal access to many routes in the western part of the area, where previously only negotiated permissive paths existed. However, with rights comes responsibility and there is still an onus on walkers to be sensitive to the needs of other land users. Much of the open land is used for the grazing of sheep and cattle, and this has implications, in particular, for the taking of dogs into the hills at certain times of year.

In addition, most of the open land borders on farmland where the lanes are narrow and inconsiderate parking or blocked gateways could cause more than just annoyance. The OS maps for the area should be consulted for the limits of Access Land, where open country is shaded yellow, while on the ground look out for the circular brown discs with the symbol of a walker against a white background.

Glossary

Common Welsh words found in the text and maps:

aber	mouth of river	*cwm*	bowl, valley	*mynydd*	mountain
allt	hillside, wood	*esgair*	ridge	*nant*	stream, valley
bach	small	*fach*	small	*ogof*	cave
blaen	source of river	*fan*	peak	*pant*	hollow, valley
brig	peak	*fawr*	big	*pen*	head, top
bryn	hill	*foel*	bald hill	*pont*	bridge
bwlch	pass	*gaer*	fort	*rhiw*	hill
cae	field	*glyn*	glen	*sgwd*	waterfall
cefn	ridge, hillside	*heol*	road	*tre, tref*	town
cerrig	stones	*llan*	church	*ty*	house
coed	wood	*llyn*	lake	*waun*	moorland, meadow
cribyn	crest	*maen*	stone		
crug	mound	*maes*	field		

Looking towards Hay Bluff from Twmpa ▶

Separated from the rest of the Beacons by the Usk Valley, these hills form the eastern part of the Brecon Beacons. The five long ridges and six steep-sided river valleys were famously described by the writer and critic Raymond Williams as the 'hand of the Black Mountains'. Although often regarded as gentler than the more western areas of the national park, the slopes actually rise to more than 800m on the highest top of Waun Fach and contain a significant amount of terrain above 600m. However, the valleys are dotted with the attractive patchwork of old field systems and still-working farms, while the towns of Abergavenny, Crickhowell and Hay-on-Wye provide easy setting-off points to the scenic backdrop of grass, bracken and heather-covered slopes. Hidden in the lanes and folds of the hillsides are the vestiges of a more populous age, routes taken by drovers and the homes of the valleys' inhabitants, past and present, including the well-known walls of Llanthony Priory in the Vale of Ewyas.

The Black Mountains

1 Black Hill and the Olchon 8
Choose a sunny day to enjoy this gem of a hill to its fullest

2 The Black Darren 10
Stride out right along one of the best sections of the majestic Welsh border

3 Twmpa and Hay Bluff 12
Enjoy the long ridges and far-reaching views on this popular round

4 The Vale of Ewyas 14
A walk of contrasts right in the heart of the Black Mountains

5 Hatterrall Hill 16
A delight of a walk from a pretty village to the heights above Llanthony Priory

6 Twyn y Gaer 18
A short but steep outing to a hillfort guarding a commanding position

7 The Skirrid 20
Take the long way around and up this much-loved peak

8 The Sugar Loaf 22
A classic outing from Abergavenny with some great views

9 Waun Fach 24
This route will take you to the highest point in the Black Mountains

10 Crug Hywel and Pen Allt-mawr 26
From Llanbedr, climb to the hillfort of Crug Hywel and the higher peaks beyond

11 A round of Cwm Sorgwm 28
Don't miss these less-walked hills which give high grazing for wild ponies

12 Llangorse Lake loop 30
Follow in ancient footsteps on a leisurely walk with plenty of wildlife

Black Hill and the Olchon

Distance 8km **Time** 2 hours 30
Terrain high moorland and a short exposed ridge with a steep start and 260m of ascent **Map** OS Explorer OL13
Access no public transport to the start

A short walk that has it all – an exposed ridge, fine views, open moorland and a hidden valley.

The Welsh name for the hill is Crib y Garth. It means 'Crest of the Ridge' and aptly describes the airy walk to be had along the sandstone outcrops. However, the hill has also come to be known locally as the Cat's Back. The reason often given for this unusual name is that, when viewed from the north or the south, the outline of the hill forms the shape of a cat arching on its haunches. Sceptics of such etymologising may put this in the same category as spotting faces in clouds which, in fact, is an ideal activity here on a summer's day when the sun has warmed the grassy sandstone ledges on top of the ridge.

From the Black Hill picnic area (GR288329) cross the stile and climb the steep bracken-covered southeast ridge ahead which soon narrows and passes over some sandstone outcrops. The reward for the rapid gain in height is, on a clear day, far-reaching views northeastwards to the Malverns, then left to the Long Mynd, the hills of Mid Wales to the north and, to the west, the heart of the Black Mountains themselves. Spread out below is a patchwork of field boundaries, some of which have been in use since humans first cultivated this area. Now you can enjoy a breezy walk

which in 2.5km reaches the triangulation point marking the plateau-like top of Black Hill (640m), complete with some black and boggy pools. If you are lucky, peregrines and ring ouzels can be spotted hereabouts and on the slopes below.

The clear path wanders northwestwards over the broad heathery ridge with views ahead to the slopes leading to Hay Bluff. After 1.3km look out for a path which bears back to the left, descending beside the infant Olchon Brook and past a ruined stone shepherd's cottage. After 500m the route enters a cleft and descends more steeply past waterfalls and rocky outcrops, down through sheep pastures and along an old walled lane to the head of the road in the valley below. Here, bear left and follow the tree-lined road for 1.75km past a number of ruined roadside cottages to reach a left turn up to the Black Hill picnic area and the start.

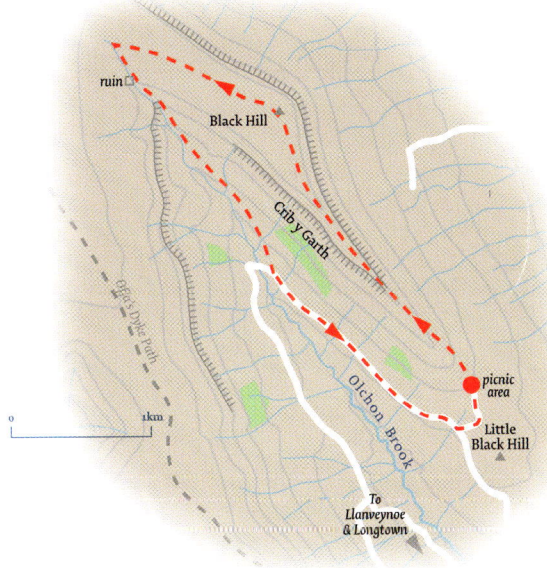

◂ The steep slopes of the Olchon Valley

The Black Darren

Distance 7.5km **Time** 2 hours 30
Terrain paths over open moorland with 290m of ascent **Map** OS Explorer OL13
Access no public transport to the start

A perfect little route for a shorter outing, but there are still long ridge-top views and even an optional scramble.

Running along the top of this ridge is the Offa's Dyke Path. It is a great route for a long-distance path to take, but the actual dyke is some miles away to the east. However, you can look, on a clear day, right into King Offa's 8th-century kingdom of Mercia, which covered most of what is now southern England. The path does follow a line decided by another king. In 1536, Henry VIII decided to challenge the power of the Lords Marcher by forming the Union of England and Wales, fixing the exact line of the boundary along Hatterrall Ridge. The Welsh language, no respecter of arbitrary boundaries, continued to be spoken on the English side of the border, in southwestern Herefordshire, until at least the 18th century.

From the Pandy to Hay-on-Wye road above Longtown, follow the signed Mountain Road for 3km through Turnant to the high parking area below the Black Darren (GR297299). Take the path (signed for Offa's Dyke Path which runs along the top of the ridge) up into the cwm that divides the Red from the Black Darren.

After 300m, bear left and up into the cleft ahead. Here, you can see the path of the landslip down the hillside which has left a short ridge exposed on the left and bands of dark rock exposed on the right. There is a choice of routes at this point. Either head up through the cleft or, for those wishing to use their hands as well, the ridge on the left gives a short and straightforward scramble. At the top of the landslip area continue to contour round underneath the rock outcrops and then circle uphill to meet a path rising from the left. Follow this path up onto the plateau-like ridge above the Black Darren until the main Offa's Dyke Path is reached.

Here, turn left and enjoy the easy terrain and extensive views, descending gently for 2km to the triangulation point at 552m above Llanthony, which lies in the valley to the west. Now descend for another 1km to reach a stone waymarker and here turn left downhill (signed for Olchon). This grassy path gives a delightful descent to the valley. After dropping down for 1km, bear left onto a byway, an old drovers' route, which contours the eastern side of the hill below Hatterrall Spring, leading in just over 1km to the small farming settlement of Turnant. Join the road here and follow it northwards for 1.2km back to the start.

◂ On Offa's Dyke Path heading south

Twmpa and Hay Bluff

Distance 16km **Time** 5 hours **Terrain** high moorland ridges; total height gain 590m **Map** OS Explorer OL13 **Access** no public transport to the start

A classic round of some of the best-loved tops in the Black Mountains and across the high Gospel Pass.

Start in the village of Capel-y-ffin, high in the Vale of Ewyas, 6.5km above Llanthony (GR254314). The name means 'Chapel of the Boundary' and the place still very much has a feeling of seclusion. As you approach from the south, it is easy to assume that the steep bulk of Darren Lwyd blocks any further progress up the valley. However, there has long been a through-route here – Gerald of Wales allegedly came this way in the 12th century and by his preaching gave the name to Bwlch-yr-Efengyl, Gospel Pass, above the hamlet. The Church of St Mary itself is tiny and has a lopsided belltower and some ancient yews surrounding it. There is a gravestone carved by the artist Eric Gill, who lived in The Monastery a little above the hamlet for a few years in the 1920s, where there is another, now ruined, chapel, and just over the Afon Honddu is a third one. So many chapels for so few people.

Walk up the lane for 250m and take the field-path on the left which goes up to and through the grounds of a cottage. Beyond, follow the path uphill for 250m before bearing right and climbing the steep slope of Darren Lwyd on a zigzagging path onto the ridge itself

TWMPA AND HAY BLUFF

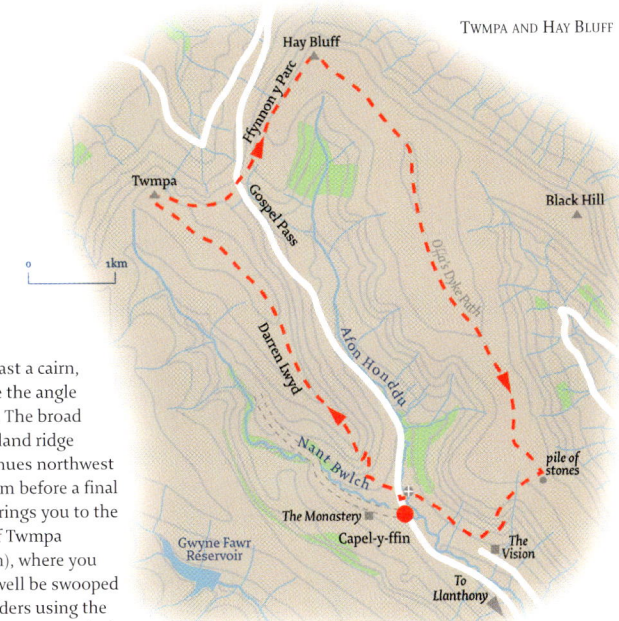

and past a cairn, where the angle eases. The broad moorland ridge continues northwest for 3km before a final rise brings you to the top of Twmpa (68om), where you may well be swooped by gliders using the escarpment's updraft.

Here, bear sharp right on a clear path which sweeps down to Gospel Pass, with views into Mid Wales. Cross the road and head up again, fairly steeply at first, for 1.7km to the triangulation point marking the top of Hay Bluff (677m). Turn right onto a laid path, which now keeps your feet dry, across the boggy moorland. After 850m pass an Offa's Dyke Path stone marker and climb the short slope ahead, after which the clear path, paved with stone slabs or laid gravel, bears round to the south. Now descend for 2.5km to a low point before another small rise to the top of a broad lump. From here continue, descending a little, for 400m to a small pile of stones, currently located where a section of stone slabs end.

Turn right here onto a narrow grassy path which descends southwest and, as the angle steepens, zigzags down the bracken-covered slopes of the cwm to a stile. Turn left over the stile down through a patch of woodland to the lane just along from The Vision, a former farm. Now turn right up the lane, which after 150m becomes a track and starts to descend. Continue across the Nant y Ffin and four small fields, where a track leads you down past the two chapels, over the Afon Honddu, and back to Capel-y-ffin.

◀ Vale of Ewyas

The Vale of Ewyas

Distance 14km **Time** 4 hours 30
Terrain valley paths and open moorland; total height gain 450m
Map OS Explorer OL13 **Access** no public transport to the start

From valley bottoms to high moorland ridges, all set against the backdrop of the iconic ruins of Llanthony Priory.

Start from the car park by Llanthony Priory (GR289278). Llanthony Priory is dedicated to St David, commemorated in the original name Llanddewi Nant Honddu, or St David's in the Valley of the Honddu. He apparently had his first leek here. Today it is a tourist spot managed by Cadw, but back in the 12th century it was a harsh place to live and most of the Augustinian monks soon fled to found a second priory at Gloucester. There is also a third Llanthony. This one, known as Llanthony Tertia or simply as The Monastery, was founded in 1870 by the Reverend Leycester Lyne a little up the valley at Capel-y-ffin. Lyne took the name Father Ignatius and preached a type of bizarre medieval asceticism. There were some Lourdes-like visions of St Mary in 1880 in the grounds, but the foundation did not long survive Lyne's death in 1908.

Walk back past the entrance to the priory and cross the field to the road to Capel-y-ffin. Bear right up past the Half Moon Hotel and in another 50m at the junction bear right. Follow the narrow hedge-lined lane for 1km to a gate. Here, continue ahead along a bridleway for 750m before joining another lane for 1.25km to Garn Farm, where the tarmac gives out. Continue in the same direction,

THE VALE OF EWYAS

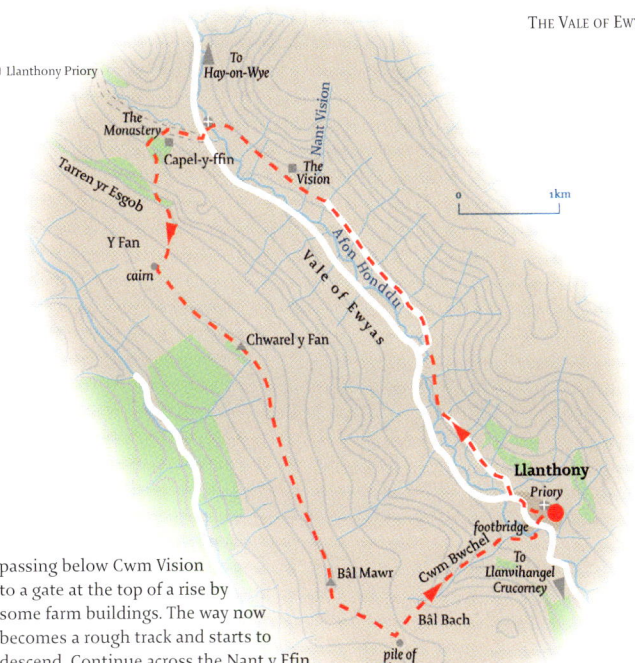

passing below Cwm Vision to a gate at the top of a rise by some farm buildings. The way now becomes a rough track and starts to descend. Continue across the Nant y Ffin and four small fields, where a track leads you down past two chapels, over the Afon Honddu, into Capel-y-ffin.

Bear left along the road over the bridge and turn right up the lane for 400m, passing below The Monastery. Take the bridleway on the left which leads up through the pony trekking centre to a gate onto the open hillside. The bridleway now heads up and then over a flatter area before zigzagging up to the lip of the steep escarpment of Tarren yr Esgob. From here a boggy path rises more gently to the ridge, marked by a cairn.

Here, bear left up the narrowing ridge to Chwarel y Fan (679m), beyond which the path leads SSE for 2.5km to the triangulation point on Bal Mawr. Now descend southeast for 600m to the large pile of stones marking the crosspaths at Bal Bach. Turn left to descend on the clear path into Cwm Bwchel. After 1.4km pass some farm buildings into the fields beyond and bear right with the path across the stream, which should now be followed for 400m to a footbridge, across which a lane leads up to the road at Llanthony. A dogleg left and then right takes you back to the priory.

Hatterrall Hill

Distance 13km **Time** 4 hours **Terrain** open moorland and valley paths with an ascent of 470m **Map** OS Explorer OL13
Access no public transport to the start

A chance to stride out on much-loved Hatterrall Hill before ambling back over fields and through woods.

The walk starts from the narrow lane above the church in Cwmyoy, where there is room for a few cars to park (GR299234). If it is a popular time of year for walking or a Sunday when there is a service, it may be better to start this walk from the car park at Llanthony Priory.

Take the sunken lane above the church (signed for Graig) uphill to a gate and signboard. Here, turn right and follow the path below craggy outcrops and then north into Cwm Lau for 1.3km, passing the restored 16th-century farmhouse of Ty-hwnt-y-bwlch, which is perhaps well named as 'House-beyond-the-Pass'.

At the head of the cwm, cross the stream and bear left uphill to a drystone wall which leads up onto the open hillside. As the slope levels out the path becomes indistinct, but by heading north over the heather you will soon pick up Offa's Dyke Path coming in from the right near the top of Hatterrall Hill (531m).

Now the broad ridge descends gently northwards for 1.2km, with great views left into Wales and right into England. At a stone marker 200m beyond the ridge's low point turn left downhill for Llanthony. After 1.6km, look out for a fingerpost, where a path leads down to the left across fields and through woodland to Llanthony Priory.

To continue, go down the lane beyond the priory to the road and turn left.

HATTERRALL HILL

◀ St Martin's Church, Cwmyoy

Around the bend, in 300m, take the path off left over fields for 1.5km towards the buildings of Maes-y-Beran. From here, continue southwards down the valley through the ruins of The Weild and on for another 1km to the point where a footbridge crosses the Afon Honddu.

Here, do not cross the bridge but continue ahead, up through some woodland, across two fields and through the farm of Daren-uchaf. The path now passes to the left of the house beyond and then up to the left for 350m to a T-junction below the cliffs of Hatterrall Hill. Turn right and pass above the buildings of Daren-isaf and, 100m further on, pick up an old tree-lined lane, which descends round the southern side of the hill to the gate and signboard a little above Cwmyoy.

Cwmyoy's church is well known for its tower which leans up the hill and its nave which leans down the hill. Being built, along with most of the village, on the spoilheap of an ancient landslide has created this anomaly. It is also on the pilgrimage route, via Llanthony Priory, to St David's in Pembrokeshire and this may account for the story that here too, as on the Skirrid above Abergavenny, the mountain was rocked by an earthquake at the time of the crucifixion. You can explore the trench and crags that tower above the village, though in recent years bracken has become even more invasive.

Twyn y Gaer

Distance 5.5km **Time** 1 hour 45
Terrain woodland and moorland paths with an ascent of 300m
Map OS Explorer OL13 **Access** no public transport to the start

Step back to the time of the Celts on this short outing to Twyn y Gaer Iron Age fort, before enjoying the pub that lies at its foot.

Start from the car park just north of The Queen's Head Inn above the settlement of Stanton on the road to Llanthony (GR311221). Walk westwards up the steep lane for 450m and take the broad forest ride which bears off right through a barrier. The ride rises gently through pleasant deciduous woodland for 700m, with glimpses of Hatterrall Hill and its impressive landslip through the trees over to the right.

Now the path levels off with conifers on either side and in another 700m passes over a crosspaths (at this point ignore the overgrown path on the left to Gaer Ridge) before descending slightly round a right-hand bend. Here, look out for a bridleway and fingerpost on the left, also signed Gaer Ridge. Follow this bridleway uphill to a wooden gate. Bear left up a field and through a metal field-gate to the trackway beyond, running along Gaer Ridge.

Turn left onto the trackway, which has a clear view ahead to the slopes of Twyn y Gaer (427m). After 350m bear right off the main trackway onto a grassy path that climbs between bracken and then gorse bushes to the top of the hill, marked by a cairn. On a clear day there are panoramic views from here back into the Black Mountains, round into Herefordshire and south to the nearer hills of the Skirrid and the Sugar Loaf.

Excavations of the site were led by a local archaeologist, Leonard Allan Probert, who was elected a fellow of the Society of Antiquaries in 1977 and who had also previously located a Roman fort at Gobannium, modern Abergavenny. At Twyn y Gaer he revealed, for the first time in South Wales, the complex history of an Iron Age hillfort, which was begun in about 450BC as a promontory fort and enclosed by a palisade for the keeping of stock animals. The finds on the site ranged from pottery to metal objects of iron and copper, brooches and glass beads. Now, among the bracken and gorse, you can still see the banks and ditches and what is thought to be the fort's entrance on the eastern side.

To descend, circle down through the earthen banks on the hill's eastern side and then left along a fence to rejoin the trackway lower down. Here, turn right through a gate and along the track for 300m to the top of the lane. This leads down, steeply in places, to return to the start after 1.3km.

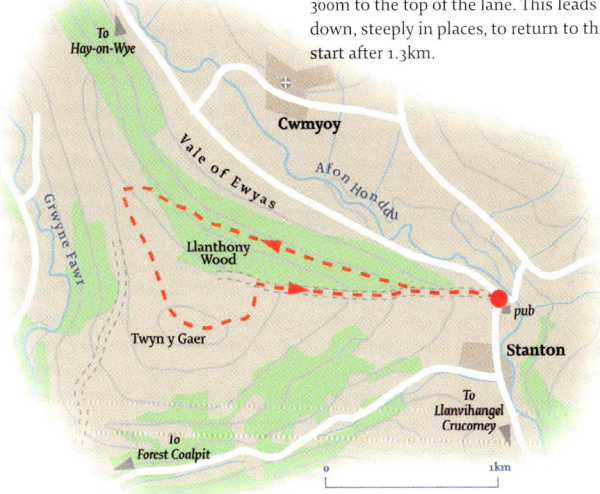

The Skirrid

Distance 5km **Time** 1 hour 45
Terrain woodland and open slopes with one steep ascent; total height gain 300m
Map OS Explorer OL13 **Access** no public transport to the start

Small but perfectly formed, Ysgyryd Fawr, or The Skirrid, is one of the best little mountains there is.

Start from the National Trust car park 3km northeast of Abergavenny beside the B4521 (GR328164). From the west end of the car park, take the track heading directly uphill to a gate. Beyond the gate, head straight up into the woodland and keep to the waymarked path that weaves uphill, ignoring forestry tracks on either side. This path brings you, in 400m, to a gate in a stone wall before a substantial wooded crag.

Here, turn right up a clear track beside the wall and in 100m, at a fork, ignore the path heading up to the left and keep ahead on the more level track that soon bears to the left around the south side of the hill. The path now narrows, following a fenceline and old stone wall on the right as it contours the eastern slopes of the hill. In summer, you may find the path a little overgrown by the encroaching bracken, brambles and gorse, though the views eastwards into Herefordshire and Monmouthshire are stunning – the two near hills visible are the Graig and Garway

Hill with its communications mast.

After 1.5km the path starts to curve left round the northern edge of the hill. As it does so, look out for a stile in the fence and, at this point, bear left up a narrower path that heads straight up the steep northern slope of the hill. This soon brings you to the triangulation point at the top of Ysgyryd Fawr (486m), with the reward of some fine views.

There are three explanations for the formation of the notch at the north end of the hill. According to local folklore, Jack O' Kent is responsible – in a contest with the Devil himself he was digging around for some big stones to hurl as far as he could. They landed in the village of Trellech, 19km away in the Wye Valley. Early Christians claim the hill was split at the same time as the crucifixion, when also the veil of the Temple of Jerusalem was sundered. Geologists, rather predictably, cite evidence of a landslip or earthquake.

Whatever the truth, soil from the site used to be scattered on coffins at local burials, and the nearby village of Llanvihangel Crucorney commemorates the appearance of the archangel Michael here or on The Skirrid itself, where there was once also a chapel dedicated to him.

To descend, follow the splendid undulating ridge southwards, which all too soon ends as it steepens briefly, before weaving a way down through a small crag to emerge on the track just above the gate in the wall encountered on the way up. From here, follow the outward route back down to the start.

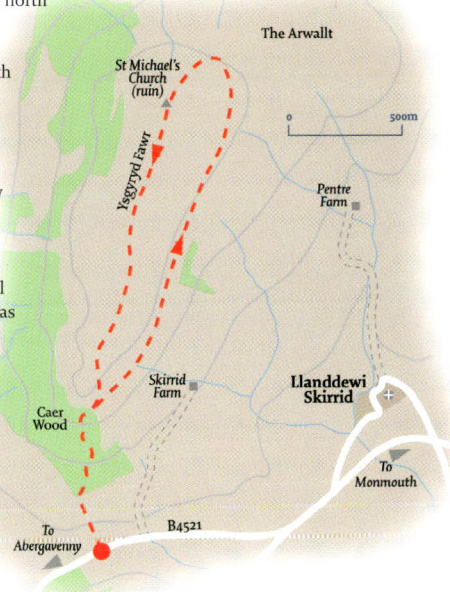

◀ The Skirrid from the northwest

The Sugar Loaf

Distance 12km **Time** 4 hours
Terrain fields, woodland and moorland paths with an ascent of 550m
Map OS Explorer OL13 **Access** buses to Abergavenny from Brecon, Newport and Hereford and trains from Hereford, Newport and Cardiff

Your feet will be just itching for a chance to tackle this peak that towers so enticingly above Abergavenny.

Abergavenny often points to its long history as a market and border town, site of the Roman fort of Gobannium, stronghold of the Lords Marcher, sacked by Owain Glyndwr and Parliamentarian forces, and its later prosperity owing to its proximity to the coal-mining districts of South Wales. But it was once equally famed for its goats. Their hair was used in the production of highly-prized white wigs and their milk was thought to be a cure for consumption.

From the centre of Abergavenny, by the war memorial, cross Park Road and go up Pen-y-Pound road for 800m, keeping to the left side to stay on Pen-y-Pound where the road forks at traffic lights. Continue past the secondary school and up the hill to a crossroads. Turn left along Chain Road and at the next crossroads turn right uphill to find a path that runs

THE SUGAR LOAF

parallel to the road (signed for the Sugar Loaf). After 250m the path bears left over a field up to a farm and a lane. Continue ahead up the lane and in 400m, at a fork, where the lane becomes a track, bear left below some houses and into the woodland reserve of Deri-Fach (Little Oaks). You soon reach a slab footbridge over a stream and a path beside it on the left.

Follow this narrowing path up through the wooded St Mary's Vale for 1.5km, ignoring paths off left or right. Some 300m after it emerges from the trees, look out for a crosspaths. Here, turn right onto a path which initially leads up through bracken and beside a small side-stream and then over the open hillside to the top of the Sugar Loaf (596m) itself.

Descend the path down the hill's initially steep northeastern side for 200m. Then bear right to avoid continuing along the hill's broad northeast ridge and, in another 100m, bear left towards the top of the wooded valley ahead. The path curves around the top of this valley, where bilberry pickers often gather in summer, and then turns southeastwards. Follow the main path along the crest of Deri ridge for 2.5km, with views to the Blorenge and the Skirrid, over the high point and down between two patches of woodland just before the end of the ridge at Twyn-yr-allt.

From here, descend ahead through woodland, where the path soon swings right and circles down to the bottom of the wood. Now bear right for 300m to a wooden gate onto a lane. Turn left, go around the bend and descend the lane (or use the parallel field edge path on the right) to reach the top of Pen-y-Pound road again, where the outward route leads back down into the town.

◀ The eastern slopes of the Sugar Loaf

Waun Fach

Distance 17km **Time** 5 hours 30
Terrain remote high moorland ridges and secluded valley; total height gain 650m
Map OS Explorer OL13 **Access** no public transport to the start

Dark and peaty ridges lead to the highest ground in the Black Mountains, but the descent to the valley is on the smoothest of grassy mountain paths.

Start from the small parking lay-by beside the road, 5km above the village of Llanbedr north of Crickhowell (GR230248). Return down the road for 1.2km and take the lane heading left down the hill above Cwm Farm. After 50m turn left onto a footpath over a bridge across a stream and, 50m beyond this, bear right uphill onto a broad track, which leads in 300m to a track junction. Turn left along this track as it contours above the woodland before going right through a field gate in another 300m. Take the path up over fields alongside an old hedgerow and above Nantyrychain Farm, after 650m passing into a conifer plantation.

Once through the plantation, bear right up across a forestry track and take the path through bracken on the right side of the cwm and up onto the broad ridge. Now turn left and follow the path, boggy in places, along the ridge for 4km, over the rounded top of Pen Twyn Mawr and up to the cairn on Pen y Gadair Fawr (Big Chair Hill, 800m). The route now descends to a low point before bearing a few degrees west onto the slopes of Waun Fach (810m) itself. Restoration work to reduce erosion and restore important upland peat bogs has taken place here as on many of the national park's hills. The final approach to the top of this hill still requires careful navigation in mist.

From Waun Fach descend southwest and then south along the narrowing ridge of Pen Trumau to reach the cairned low

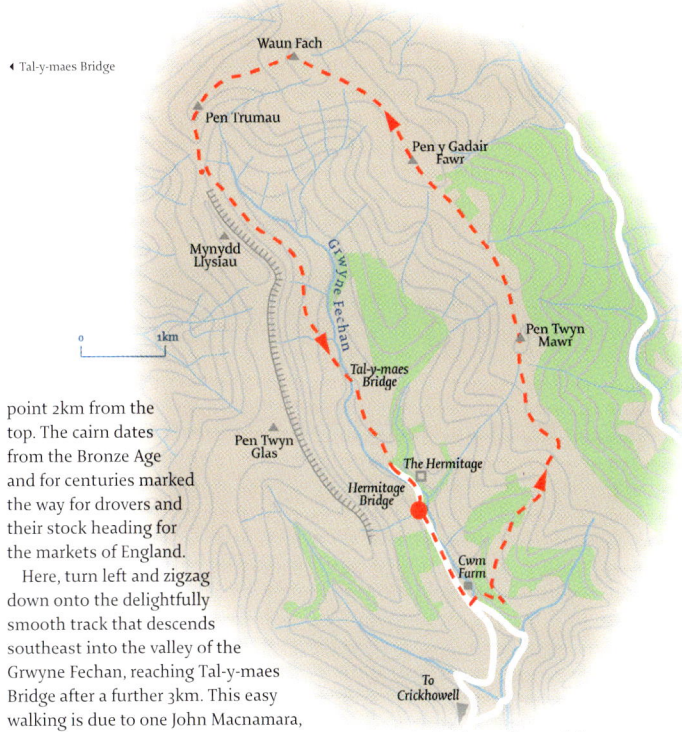

◀ Tal-y-maes Bridge

point 2km from the top. The cairn dates from the Bronze Age and for centuries marked the way for drovers and their stock heading for the markets of England.

Here, turn left and zigzag down onto the delightfully smooth track that descends southeast into the valley of the Grwyne Fechan, reaching Tal-y-maes Bridge after a further 3km. This easy walking is due to one John Macnamara, an 18th-century landowner with a colourful reputation who has a number of apocryphal stories attached to him. One such myth is that he had the carriage road built from his estate in the Rhiangoll to the west over Pen Trumau pass and down to his now ruined house at The Hermitage in order to visit a mistress he kept at the secluded property.

Cross the bridge and turn right up over fields, in 600m passing a stand of pines, where the path becomes a track and descends to the Hermitage Bridge. Turn right over the bridge, with the Grwyne Fechan flowing fast below, and head down the lane for 500m, passing the ruins of The Hermitage on the left across the stream, to return to the start.

Crug Hywel and Pen Allt-mawr

Distance 14.5km **Time** 4 hours 30
Terrain high moorland tops and ridges with some steep ascent; total height gain 670m **Map** OS Explorer OL13
Access no public transport to the start

History and geology meet to make this the most interesting of high-level rounds.

Start from the village of Llanbedr, 3km north of Crickhowell (GR239203). Walk west out of the village up the lane to the T-junction. Turn right along the road for 500m and take the path off left, signed Perth-y-Pia and Table Mountain (the English name for Crug Hywel). Climb steeply past the 18th-century farmhouse onto the open slopes beyond and up to the former hillfort of Crug Hywel, which gives its name to the town below.

Now turn northwards across a dip and climb the ridge ahead, over a nose of rock, beyond which the path becomes less steep and heads a few degrees west to reach the triangulation pillar on Pen Cerrig-calch (701m), 2km from the fort. The plateau here, as the name of the hill suggests, is covered with fractured blocks of limestone (*calch* being Welsh for 'lime'), all the more striking amongst the dark peat.

For the next 2.5km, the route descends northwest along the broad ridge, crossing a dip marked by a pile of stones, before hugging the right-hand escarpment and climbing gently to Pen Allt-mawr (719m) at the northern end of the ridge, a

magnificent point for taking in the view to Waun Fach and west to the Central Beacons.

A steep but short descent along the hill's north ridge leads to a broad low point, beyond which the path bears round to the northeast. Here, head for the small rounded top of Pen Twyn Glas (perhaps *glas*, 'green', because of the change to grassy terrain).

Leaving the main ridge, which sweeps northwards up to Waun Fach, drop southeast on the long grassy ridge for 2.5km, past an area of old quarries, to a prominent cairn. Continue down the ridge, over a stile and into fields, where the path becomes a stony track. At a fork in the track bear right through the gate and, in 50m, drop steeply left down a field, following the marker posts, and at the bottom head left to the lane.

Turn right over the bridge and follow the pleasant lane, uphill at first and then down the valley of the Grwyne Fechan for 1.75km, where an even narrower unsigned lane leads left back down to Llanbedr.

Nearby Crickhowell is the birthplace of Sir George Everest, the Surveyor-General of India, who had his name attached to the highest mountain in the world. He was born just west of the town, at what is now The Manor Hotel. At the bottom of its drive, where the traffic speeds by on the A40, are a collection of old stones, the remnants of a Neolithic burial chamber which was composed of rocks much older than the Himalayas.

◀ *Above the valley of the Grwyne Fechan*

A round of Cwm Sorgwm

Distance 13.5km **Time** 4 hours 30
Terrain moorland paths with some steep sections; total height gain 780m
Map OS Explorer OL13 **Access** no public transport to the start

These outliers of the Black Mountains massif are easily missed, but are a real treat with great views.

Start from Pont Waun Fach (GR183262). There is very limited parking at a lay-by next to the phonebox on the minor road at the junction with the A479, or further up the minor road. Walk up the minor road, past the old Waun Fach Forge, for 1km and, just beyond a left fork, take the footpath on the right into fields to reach sheep pens and the start of Access Land.

Here, make for the top left corner of this steep field, which has been enclosed from the open hillside. Cross the top fence and bear right on a distinct sheep track for 200m before heading left up to the crest of the ridge. Now follow the ridge northwest for 2.5km – it soon levels out and broadens, giving an airy walk to the triangulation point marking the top of Mynydd Troed (609m).

The path descending the hill's southwest ridge to the head of Cwm

A round of Cwm Sorgwm

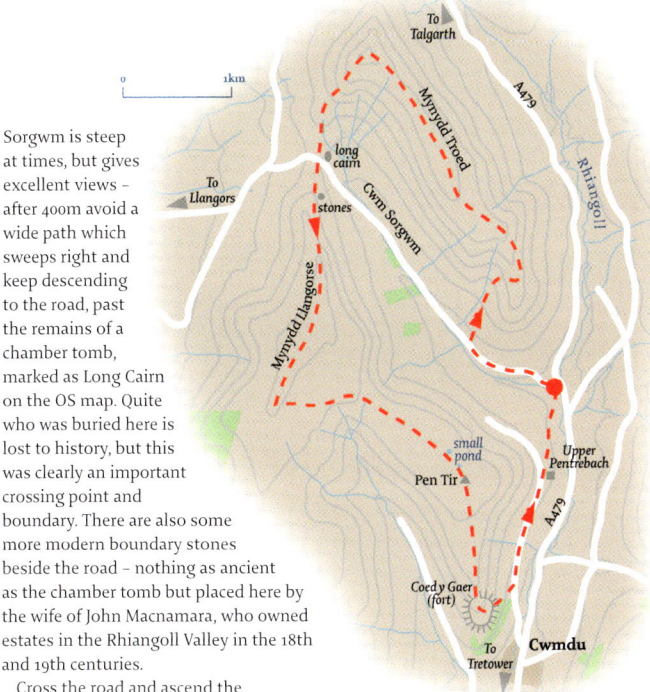

Sorgwm is steep at times, but gives excellent views – after 400m avoid a wide path which sweeps right and keep descending to the road, past the remains of a chamber tomb, marked as Long Cairn on the OS map. Quite who was buried here is lost to history, but this was clearly an important crossing point and boundary. There are also some more modern boundary stones beside the road – nothing as ancient as the chamber tomb but placed here by the wife of John Macnamara, who owned estates in the Rhiangoll Valley in the 18th and 19th centuries.

Cross the road and ascend the narrowing ridge ahead, with a steep drop left into Cwm Sorgwm. As the ground levels out, keep to the path bearing to the right for 1.2km over the high point of the Mynydd Llangorse plateau and on to the slightly lower triangulation point.

From here, head east towards the top of the cwm and, just beyond an upright stone marker and fingerpost, pick up the path that heads over Pen Tir. Keep to the high ground of the plateau and after 1km reach a small lake. Now proceed south for 1.5km down a gradually steepening ridge to the fenceline.

Here, turn left past a ruined cottage and descend the old track to the lane. A left turn along this pleasant lane above the Rhiangoll brings you in 1km to a stone stile by a fingerpost (50m past the buildings of Upper Pentrebach). Bear right into fields here and follow the waymarked path in a northerly direction to join the road at Pont Waun Fach.

◀ Looking back at Mynydd Troed across Cwm Sorgwm

Llangorse Lake loop

Distance 16.5km **Time** 5 hours
Terrain moorland, fields and lakeside paths; total height gain 570m
Map OS Explorer OL13 **Access** bus to Bwlch from Abergavenny and Brecon

A real hands-in-pockets walk, but it would be a good idea to take a pair of binoculars for gazing at the wildlife attracted by the lake.

Start from the western end of the village of Bwlch, where there is some roadside parking in a small lay-by, on the B4560, 50m past the village hall. Walk back up to the shop, a former tollhouse, and turn left along the main road into the village centre. At the top of the rise, turn left up a narrow lane between houses and, after 150m, bear left to follow the route of the Beacons Way up onto the open hillside.

After the initial climb to a cairn, a clear track continues northwards along the undulating ridge of the Mynydd Llangorse (515m) to a crosspaths after 2km, where the Beacons Way bears right. Here, continue ahead uphill and in 750m bear left, off the main track, up past the triangulation point and on across the plateau to the high point.

Just past the high point, at a crosspaths, bear left down the western slope of the hill. In 500m, the path turns back sharp left and descends into the cwm to a gate and bridleway crosspaths lower down. Go through the gate and along the field edge to pick up a holloway down to a lane. Here, turn left down past Llangorse Multi Activity Centre to the B4560. Bear right along the road for 100m and then take a footpath on the right over fields.

Llangorse Lake loop

Follow the right-hand edge of the large third field as it turns left (northwest), and continue over more fields to reach a lane. Turn left down to the B4560 and then right to head into the village of Llangors.

In the centre of the village, just before the Baptist Chapel, turn left onto a footpath which leads across fields to the north of Llangorse Lake. Cross the road leading to the sailing club and head west over the Common to a footbridge.

Reed-fringed Llangorse Lake, or Llyn Syfaddan, is one of the largest pieces of water in Wales. In the 1860s it emerged that there had been a crannog, or man-made island, here and in 1925 an ancient and well-preserved log-boat, or dug-out canoe, was found by a local. Dated at over 1000 years old, it now lies in pride of place at Y Gaer in Brecon.

Head left over fields for 1km around the western side of the lake, before bearing right up past Ty Mawr Farm and doglegging left, then right onto its drive and up to the road.

Here, dogleg right, then left up past Llangasty Hall, where there is a useful information board, onto the bridleway (muddy in places), which leads up to the top of Allt yr Esgair (393m). Descend the far side of the hill for 1.2km to the point where the path bears left down a sunken way between fields to the main A40. Turn left along the verge back into Bwlch.

◂ On the ridge of the Mynydd Llangorse

On the southern edge of the national park is an area of limestone hills, completely different in character from the rest of the Brecon Beacons, whose underlying geology is predominantly old red sandstone. The effect on the landscape is dramatic. The limestone supports very different habitats for wildlife and the terrain is pockmarked by the dips and depressions of sinkholes, indicators of far more extensive cave systems that stretch for miles underground.

At the surface, there are former quarries on the escarpments overlooking the town of Crickhowell, while the higher moorland gives some tough walking on slopes that lead to the former mining areas of the valleys around Blaenavon, now designated as a World Heritage Site.

One of the best places to see this geological change is the Clydach Gorge, west of Abergavenny. Here, you can literally walk through geological time and glimpse the rocks of ages past, from the red sandstones at the bottom, rising to the younger pale grey limestones, ironstone and the coal measures underlayed by millstone grit nearer the surface.

Old mine workings on the slopes above Blaenavon ▶

The Llangattock and Llangynidr Hills

1 The Blorenge 34
After a steep climb, walk back through industrial time above the town of Abergavenny

2 Blaenavon and Mynydd Coety 36
There's much to delay you on this moorland round above the former mining town of Blaenavon

3 Clydach Gorge 38
A chance to glimpse the industrial and geological past in and above this impressive gorge

4 Craig y Cilau 40
A short outing full of interest above the village of Llangattock

5 Cwm Claisfer and the Chartist Cave 42
Seek out a high moorland meeting place on a tough little outing

6 Tor y Foel 44
Small but perfectly formed, an ideal walk for a summer's evening

The Blorenge

Distance 13km **Time** 4 hours 30
Terrain old tramroad, high moorland and canal towpath with an ascent of 500m
Map OS Explorer OL13 **Access** bus to Llanfoist from Abergavenny where there are trains from Hereford, Newport and Cardiff

Follow an old tramroad into the area's industrial past before traversing this moorland hill and finding the picturesque nature reserve of The Punchbowl.

Start from Llanfoist Crossing car park at the western end of Llanfoist (GR286133). Cross the road and take the lane (signed for the Blorenge) up past St Faith's Church, whose churchyard holds the tomb of the ironmaster Crawshaw Bailey, and through Llanfoist Wharf tunnel under the Monmouthshire and Brecon Canal.

Now climb steeply up the former tramroad inclines through woodland and onto the open hillside beyond (ignore paths to Pen-y-graig and Garnddyrys). Keep climbing straight up into Cwm Craf beyond the topmost stile to a T-junction with the line of the old tramroad.

Thomas Hill's Tramroad from Blaenavon to Llanfoist was completed in 1817 and passes for more than 2km through Pwll-du Tunnel, at the time one of the world's longest for a horse-drawn railway, and then on to the forge at Garnddyrys, where pig iron was converted into wrought iron. From here, it contours the Blorenge to the unfeasibly steep inclines on the hill's northern side, down which the trucks were lowered for their

THE BLORENGE

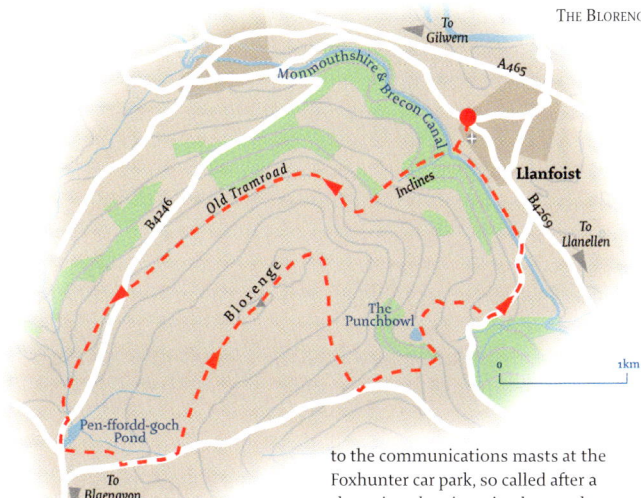

cargo to be loaded onto canal barges for onward transportation.

Turn right onto the old tramroad and follow it around the bracken-covered slopes of the Blorenge for 2.5km to meet the B4246 just below the site of the forge at Garnddyrys. Dogleg left for 100m, then right at the bend onto the signed Iron Mountain Trail and through an area of slagheaps. Here, pick up the line of the tramroad again which contours round the left side of the valley for 1km to the stream at the head of steep-sided Cwm Ifor (avoid paths leading off downhill).

Cross the stream and in 100m turn sharp left uphill (signed for Keeper's Pond) to meet the road again, beyond which lies this body of water, also known as Pen-ffordd-goch Pond. From the pond's southern end, a path leads to the road up to the communications masts at the Foxhunter car park, so called after a champion showjumping horse whose grave lies 100m northwards. Beyond the grave, bear right to pick up the main path to the summit of the Blorenge (561m).

Now continue northeast for 750m to descend to a brick hut perched on the edge of the lip of Cwm Craf. Turn right along a clear track and in 350m bear left at a fork to descend to the road. Here go left (signed for Llanfoist) onto a wide bridleway which soon descends, forking left after 400m through a gateway. The track now continues to descend through woodland to the lake of The Punchbowl.

Continue past the lake for 400m and then turn right over a stile and down the field to a drive. Turn right and descend for 200m to a corrugated barn. Pass left of the barn, then immediately right down the field to a lane. Go left downhill to the canal, where a left turn onto its towpath leads in 900m to Llanfoist Wharf.

◀ Summit plateau of the Blorenge

THE LLANGATTOCK AND LLANGYNIDR HILLS

Blaenavon and Mynydd Coety

Distance 8km **Time** 3 hours
Terrain old railway line and rough open moorland with an ascent of 300m
Map OS Explorer OL13 **Access** bus to Blaenavon from Pontypool and Newport

Discover Blaenavon's industrial past on this moorland circuit through the old mining areas that surround the town.

Start from the World Heritage Centre in the middle of Blaenavon and walk up the road for 100m, turning left just before Kennard Court to follow a walkway down to and across a grassy field to a roadbridge over the Afon Lwyd. Turn left over this bridge and climb the zigzagging Forge Side Road for 300m until you cross the old railway line, where a right turn will take you down onto the cycle track that now runs alongside it. This traffic-free route heads northwest for 2.5km, crossing over the road leading to the Big Pit National Coal Museum and doglegging right, then left to pass Garn Lakes before reaching its end at the road near The Whistle Inn.

Here, turn left over the bridge, past the wonderfully-positioned pub and up to the end of the road. Continue southwards past a ruined building on the clear track (signed to the Common) that makes a rising traverse up the side of the hill ahead. In 500m, cross a stile onto the open moorland and then go over the line of an old tramway that contours the hill. Beyond it is a climb to gain another 80m

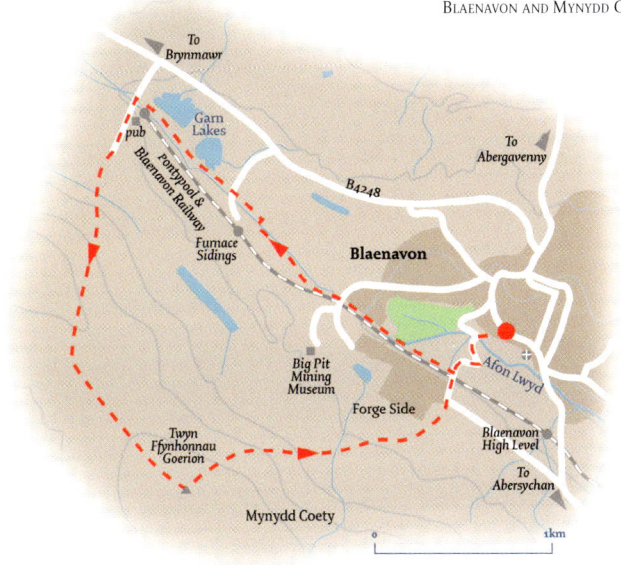

in height and reach the path's high point.

The going is now much tougher over the heather that covers the plateau, with paths that never quite seem to head in the right direction, and it can be confusing in poor visibility. The best approach is to take your time and head straight for the broad top of Mynydd Coety (grid bearing 148 degrees for 1km), initially descending across a shallow dip. From the high point (578m) of the very broad top, descend due east down grass and heather slopes to the level of the old tramway to pick up a clear path coming in above it from the right.

Take this path, which now heads ENE for 350m to a ruin, where it bears slightly to the right. The path runs along the top of a boggy fenceline and under some old wooden pylons to a gate, beyond which a track leads down to the top of Forge Side Road and the old railway line. From here, the outward route can be retraced into Blaenavon.

You can't visit Blaenavon, however, without visiting the Big Pit Museum. For decades in the 19th and 20th centuries, Big Pit was the main colliery in the town, employing more than 1000 men. Sunk in the 1860s, it was only finally closed in 1980. In 1983 the site became a mining museum and in 2001 it was incorporated into Amgueddfa Cymru – the National Museum of Wales. An underground guided tour is a memorable experience.

◂ Looking northwest to the Central Beacons

Clydach Gorge

Distance 10km **Time** 2 hours 30
Terrain canal towpath, woodland, lanes and an old railway line with 100m of ascent **Map** OS Explorer OL13
Access bus to Govilon from Abergavenny

Canals, rivers and old railway lines are followed on this route into the steep-sided Clydach Gorge which still houses its impressive ironworks.

The dramatic gorge cuts a deep trench through what is the northern edge of the South Wales Coalfield. As a result, the industrial sites, transport routes and the homes of the gorge's inhabitants were all squeezed together between the steep cliffs from Brynmawr to Gilwern. The ironworks at Clydach reached their heyday in the middle of the 18th century, with just this one site employing more than a thousand people. Now among the ruins you can still make out the blast furnaces and a wheel pit, but nature is slowly reclaiming the site. Indeed, the western half of the gorge has been designated a nature reserve, containing one of the few remaining native beechwoods in Wales.

The walk starts from Govilon, west of Abergavenny on the B4246. From the road junction at the west end of the village, walk up Church Lane past the inn of Tafarn y Bont to gain access to the Monmouthshire and Brecon Canal – go up steps where the road passes under the aqueduct. Turn right and follow the towpath for 2km, passing under the A465 and along the back of the houses of Gilwern, to the road at the Towpath Inn.

Cross over and continue along the towpath around the first bend. Here, descend steps on the right and then turn

CLYDACH GORGE

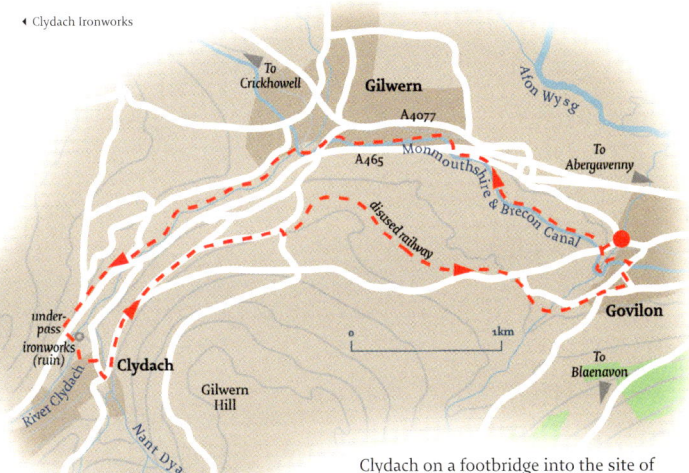

◀ Clydach Ironworks

back left through a tunnel to pass under the canal. Follow the track ahead and, just beyond the cottages, take the path on the left (signed Clydach) onto the route of the Clydach Gorge Heritage Trail. Follow this trail for 1.2km as it descends into woodland, with the noise and waterfalls of the River Clydach below, to the houses of Forge Row. Continue ahead to where the lane meets the A465.

Do not cross the busy A465 here; instead follow the road running parallel to its right to reach a fingerpost to Clydach Ironworks in 350m. Now go left down steps and through the A465 underpass. Bear right for 350m and cross the River Clydach on a footbridge into the site of Clydach Ironworks. To continue, take the path to the right of the ruins up to a road. Cross over and take the path opposite (signed Clydach Station) between houses up to the centre of Clydach village.

From here, turn left (northwards) over the bridge above a stream and proceed along the road for 1km, taking the second lane on the right, which leads up in another 500m to the old railway line. This has now been converted for the use of cyclists and walkers and in 2.5km brings you to the former station at Govilon. At the road beyond the station, turn left downhill to the canal, where a final left turn along the towpath for 150m will bring you back to the point where the canal was joined on the outward route.

Craig y Cilau

Distance 7.5km **Time** 2 hours 30
Terrain lanes, old tramroad, woodland
and fields with an ascent of 300m
Map OS Explorer OL13 **Access** bus to
Llangattock from Brecon and Abergavenny

A stiff climb leads to a peaceful walk along a limestone escarpment with plenty of wildlife to spot in this National Nature Reserve.

The cliffs of Craig y Cilau were once extensively quarried for limestone which was transported to the ironworks in Nantyglo or burned in kilns with coal to form lime with which farmers fertilised their fields. Now silent, the quarries are home to rare flora and fauna, including the lesser whitebeam. However, the area is still a draw for cavers and they are often to be seen sorting out their gear near the entrances to some of the longest cave systems in Britain – Ogof Agen Allwedd stretches underground for over 30km.

Start from the southern edge of Llangattock village above the Bethesda Chapel and roadbridge over the canal at a pair of lay-bys on Hillside Road (GR207171). If these are occupied there is roadside parking down the hill in the village. Walk up Hillside Road for 250m, with views ahead to the Llangattock Escarpment, to the bend where a track on the right leads southwest past a stone cottage to a stream, the southern branch of the Nant Onneu. Just beyond, cross a stile into woodland and climb steeply up by a fenced plantation on the left. On reaching the open hillside, continue up and

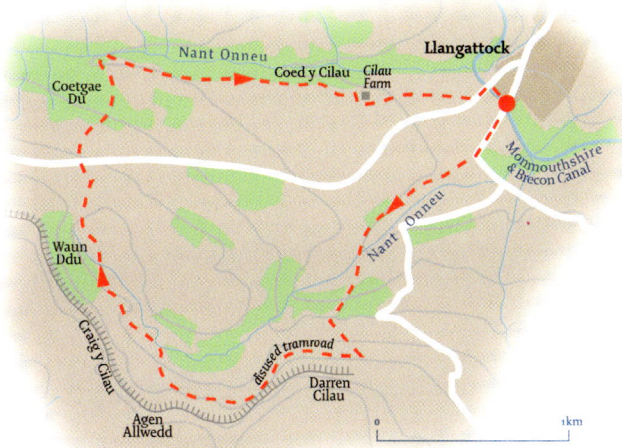

slightly left to a **disused tramroad**.

Now turn right and follow the tramroad for 1km as it contours the escarpment below cliffs, old quarry workings and the cave entrance at Eglwys Faen, with steep drops to the right and views over the Usk Valley to the Black Mountains. At a fork with a marker post, bear right (the path ahead leads to Agen Allwedd with its miles of underground passages and caves). This takes you downhill for 300m, then up over a rise and down to the raised bog of Waun Ddu. Here, keep left and climb the slope on the far side to a track by a gate. This leads left to a road in 100m.

Cross and descend the field towards the buildings of Cwm Onnau farm, seen on the other side of the valley, bearing slightly right to a gate into the woodland of Coetgae Du. Continue through the wood and then along its eastern edge down to a ford of the northern branch of the Nant Onneu. Here, do not cross the stream but turn right up and along a series of field-edge paths above the southern edge of Coed y Cilau for 1.5km to Cilau Farm. Pass to the right of the farm buildings and, on reaching a lane beyond, dogleg left, then right and head over two more fields, still in an easterly direction, to the road above Llangattock. Here, go left downhill and, in 150m, cross the canal and turn right onto its towpath. On the far side of the first bridge, climb some stone out-steps to the road just down from the lay-bys at the start.

◀ The cliffs of Craig y Cilau

Cwm Claisfer and the Chartist Cave

Distance 12km **Time** 4 hours 30
Terrain lanes, tracks, woodland and open moorland with tricky navigation; total height gain 460m **Map** OS Explorer OL13
Access bus to Llangynidr from Brecon and Abergavenny

Pick a clear day for finding the way to the high Chartist Cave, once the secret armoury of Newport rebels, on the heather and bracken moorland of the Mynydd Llangynidr.

Chartism was a liberal movement which arose in the early 1830s based around demands for a People's Charter securing the right to universal male suffrage. Welsh Chartists took direct action when 5000 of them marched in what became known as the Newport Rising of 1839. Soldiers opened fire on the crowd, leaving at least 22 dead and over 50 injured. The leaders, including John Frost, a local magistrate and then mayor of Newport, were found guilty of treason and condemned to death, though this was commuted to transportation for life to Tasmania. However, Frost was eventually pardoned in 1856 and returned to Newport as a hero.

Start from the northern end of Llangynidr, where there is a car park opposite the entrance to the village hall by the junction of the B4558 with Duffyn Road (GR155195). Walk up Duffyn Road past the church and school to the southern end of the village and, just past Mill Road, fork left along Glaisfer Road, past Sardis Church. Continue along the narrow lane uphill for 1km to a farm track on the right which leads to the stone barns of Pantllwyd. Here, keep ahead up an old sunken lane to

a gate onto open hillside, beyond which is a millennium memorial stone.

Now bear to the left and follow the rough intermittent path through the bracken which contours southwards above a drystone wall and the forestry plantation in Cwm Claisfer to cross the Nant Claisfer just above a small waterfall (GR134162).

From here, the going is pathless, through an area of sinkholes covered in heather and bracken. Use of a compass is essential in poor visibility, and at any time it is easy to become disorientated. To make for the Chartist Cave, head uphill on a grid bearing of 215 degrees for 1.3km over the time-consuming terrain. As the slope levels off, the going becomes easier – the cave entrance is just beyond a track on the east side of a rocky bluff. If you find yourself near Llyn y Garn-fawr, you have gone too far.

To return to the Nant Claisfer crossing, either retrace your steps or, for a descent easier on the knees, head ENE over the moor to pick up a path for 1km across a broad dip and then down into a bowl with a prominent sinkhole (GR138156). At a stone marking the crosspaths, turn left and head NNW back down bracken slopes to the Nant Claisfer crossing.

From here, pick a way down beside the Nant Claisfer on its right bank for 400m to a waterfall just before the Filter House, where the path squeezes to its right through some gorse bushes. A little beyond, look out for a marker post and descend left across the stream to follow its left bank, past some ruins and over a track into woodland to reach the old stone buildings at Blaen-y-cwm. The path now descends gently over fields for 750m, with the Nant Claisfer away to the right, to the lane in Cwm Claisfer. Here turn left for 2km, uphill at first and then down to join the outward route back to Llangynidr.

◂ Blaen-y-cwm

THE LLANGATTOCK AND LLANGYNIDR HILLS

Tor y Foel

Distance 8km **Time** 3 hours
Terrain canal towpath, fields and open hillside with a steep ascent of 440m up Tor y Foel **Map** OS Explorer OL13
Access no public transport to the start

A peaceful amble along a towpath leads to a stiff ascent of this shapely whaleback of a hill.

Start at the bridge in Cwmcrawnon, where the B4558 passes over the Monmouthshire and Brecon Canal, near the Coach and Horses Inn. There is space for a few cars 150m along Coed-yr-Ynys Road (signed for Bwlch) at the edge of the canal (GR146200).

The Monmouthshire and Brecon Canal, which took 15 years to build at the start of the 19th century, was once one of the main transportation links for the huge amounts of coal, iron, lime and other goods being exported from this part of Wales. Restored by British Waterways, the canal runs for 50km from Brecon to Pontypool and is now popular with narrow-boat enthusiasts, cyclists and walkers. However, along its length there is still plenty of evidence of its industrial past, in the form of bridges, wharves and locks.

Head west along the canal towpath on the route of the Usk Valley Walk for 2km,

past Llangynidr Locks to Bridge 138. Here, leave the towpath and cross the canal. Just beyond the bridge at the track junction, look out for an Usk Valley Walk marker post and turn right onto the bridleway.

The path heads uphill, at first through the undergrowth of a wood, then for 1.4km across the slopes of open fields and around the north side of Tor y Foel (551m) to the road above Talybont Reservoir. Leave the Usk Valley Walk here and turn left up the road. After 200m, look out for a path on the left which takes you straight up the grassy slopes of Tor y Foel's broad north ridge – higher up it is a little steep and unrelenting, but the reward is one of the best viewpoints in the whole of the Brecon Beacons.

The hill's east ridge makes for a delightful descent over moorland slopes to pick up a fenceline down through fields to a lane at Pen-y-beili (*beili* means 'enclosure'). Cross the lane and pick up the well-signed route of the Beacons Way. Follow this for the next 1km along the farm's drive and then down over fields in an ENE direction, before bearing left to descend through deciduous woodland and across the canal at a set of locks, where a right turn along the towpath picks up the outward route to Cwmcrawnon.

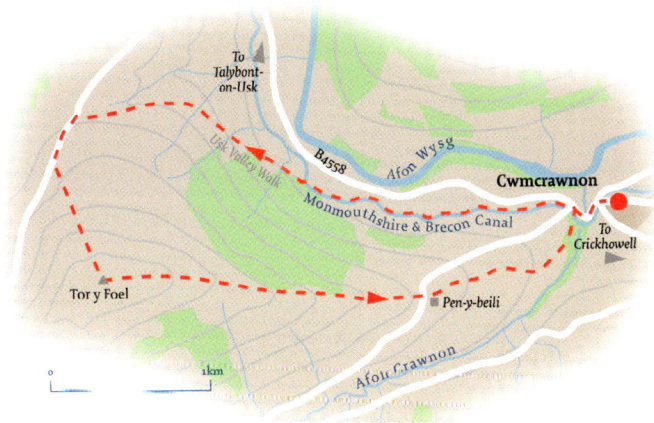

◀ The northern slopes of Tor y Foel

This is the most popular and well-known part of the national park. The town of Brecon, with its outdoor shops and cafés, is often the base for those wanting to explore the whole area. Rising above the town, the peaks of Pen y Fan, Corn Du and Cribyn are on the list of almost every walker who visits the area. And fine high peaks they are too, with a variety of ways to approach them, each presenting a very different character and surrounded by a number of lower satellites worth exploring in their own right.

Here, too, are located some of the high reservoirs, built in preceding centuries to supply the needs of the towns and cities of South Wales. Railway lines once crossed the area, transporting the commodities of iron, limestone and coal, and carrying tourists and daytrippers to see the peaks and waterfalls.

Now the tracks are mostly silent except for the passage of walkers and wheels of bikes, though one railway, the Brecon Mountain Railway, still operates seasonally above Merthyr Tydfil.

Looking north from the summit of Fan y Big ▶

The Central Beacons

1 **The Forts of Brecon** 48
Step back in time and enjoy some great views of the central peaks of the Beacons

2 **Pen y Fan and Corn Du** 50
Pick a good day to enjoy this direct approach to the highest peak in the national park

3 **Cribyn** 52
A short but satisfying route up this popular hill in the heart of the Beacons

4 **Beacons Northern Horseshoe** 54
You'll be in good company on this classic but tough round of the central peaks

5 **Fan y Big** 56
One of the best walks in the Central Beacons with the added bonus that it starts from a picturesque village

6 **Beacons Southern Horseshoe** 58
A high round of the central peaks that always feels more remote and open to the elements

7 **Talybont and Waun Rydd** 60
Stride out along an old railway line and over high moorland

8 **Pant y Creigiau** 62
A route for solitude and brooding moorland, especially in autumn

9 **Pontsticill and the Ystrad Stone** 64
A short outing full of varied scenery around Pontsticill Reservoir

THE CENTRAL BEACONS

The Forts of Brecon

Distance 10km **Time** 3 hours
Terrain lanes, bridleways, fields and open hillside; total height gain 250m
Map OS Explorer OL12 **Access** bus to Brecon from Abergavenny, Hereford and Swansea

This walk is ideal for a half-day outing or as an alternative to the popular routes of the main peaks around Brecon.

From the centre of Brecon, walk up the High Street, following signs for the cathedral. Turn left over the Afon Honddu up Priory Hill, passing the walled cathedral precinct on the right. Walk on the pavement up the hill for a further 600m and, just beyond the last houses on the left and a small stream, turn left along a narrow lane. In 700m, just before a gate, bear left at a bridleway fingerpost and climb more steeply up past a house, where the track narrows and leads to a gate onto the open hillside.

Bear right onto the grassy track which traverses the eastern side of Pen-y-Crug, an Iron Age hillfort. In 300m, a detour left will take you up to the triangulation point at the top (331m) with panoramic views. To continue, circle back to the main track and follow it down the hill's northern slope to a gate, from where the bridleway descends in 250m to the road.

Turn left along the road for 1.1km into Cradoc (a wide grass verge avoids the tarmac for much of the way). At the junction, bear right for 50m, then left along a pleasant lane (signed Aberyscir) for 1.4km to Pont-ar-Yscir. Here, just before the bridge over the Afon Ysgir, a path leads off left over a meadow, up

Beside the Afon Wysg on the outskirts of Brecon

through a stand of trees and over two fields to a house near the Roman fort of Cicucium. The fort itself lies beyond the house in the fields to the left of the farm buildings.

The fort was excavated in the 1920s by one of Britain's most eminent archaeologists, Sir Mortimer Wheeler, when he was Director of the National Museum of Wales. Using the grid system he pioneered, he uncovered what was the typical layout of a legionary camp, which would have housed about 500 legionaries. Some of what was excavated was covered over for the sake of preservation, but there are still visible stretches of walls and some of the gateways, though the northern gateway is now covered by one of the farm's stone barns. The fort stands on a road network that connected it to other forts at Gobannium (Abergavenny), Nidum (Neath) and Alabum (Llandovery).

To continue, take the gated bridleway to the left of the house. The way soon passes into a field and down into woodland. In 1km, cross a footbridge over a stream before passing to the left of the farm buildings at Pennant. From here, continue down the bridleway for a further 1.1km to Fenni-Fach Road on the outskirts of Brecon.

Here, turn left for 200m and then bear right down through a car park to pick up the walkway beside the Afon Wysg which soon leads you back into the centre of Brecon.

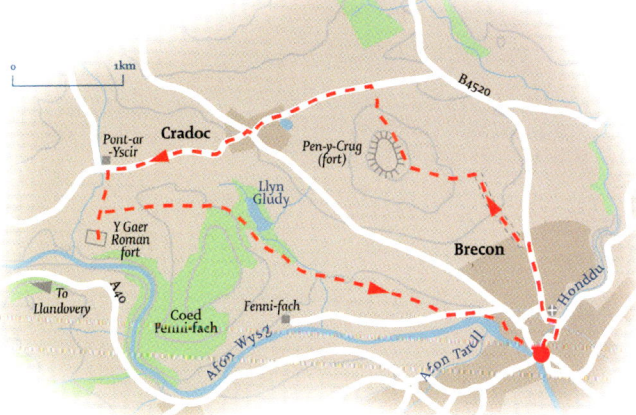

Pen y Fan and Corn Du

Distance 11km **Time** 4 hours
Terrain high open hillside and an exposed ridge up to Pen y Fan, with a steep final section; total height gain 690m
Map OS Explorer OL12 **Access** no public transport to the start

A bit of puff and a head for heights is needed for this exhilarating climb to the twin summits of Pen y Fan and Corn Du, the two highest peaks in South Wales.

Many people visit these peaks of the Brecon Beacons, not only because they form the highest tops in southern Britain but also because on a clear day the views are stunning. It has long been known that they were also crowned by ancient burial mounds. In 1989, when finally erosion threatened to destroy much of the mounds' evidence, further excavation was initiated on the cairn on Corn Du. What archaeologists have now established about the sites is that they both consisted of central burial chambers, or cists, with a double circle of overlapping sandstone slabs. It is thought that grave robbers long since removed any evidence about who might have been buried here, but it has been possible to date the construction of both cairns to around 2000BC.

Start from the car park in Cwm Gwdi (GR025248). Walk up the tarmac track to the top of the parking area and

Pen y Fan and Corn Du

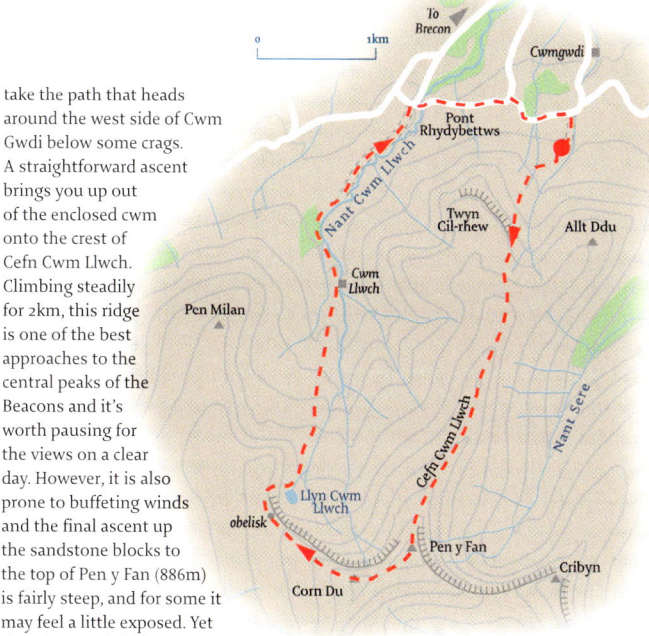

take the path that heads around the west side of Cwm Gwdi below some crags. A straightforward ascent brings you up out of the enclosed cwm onto the crest of Cefn Cwm Llwch. Climbing steadily for 2km, this ridge is one of the best approaches to the central peaks of the Beacons and it's worth pausing for the views on a clear day. However, it is also prone to buffeting winds and the final ascent up the sandstone blocks to the top of Pen y Fan (886m) is fairly steep, and for some it may feel a little exposed. Yet there is no real difficulty and the reward is to emerge directly onto the highest peak in southern Britain.

To continue, descend southwest around the rim of Cwm Llwch and make a further short ascent up to Corn Du (873m). From here, care should be taken, especially in poor visibility, to head northwest down Craig Cwm Llwch (rather than NNW where there is **no descent route** but, owing to people peering over the cliffs, there may appear to be the start of one). Follow the path that keeps to the rim of the cwm and, once past the old memorial stone to the young boy Tommy Jones, keep descending to the right to Llyn Cwm Llwch, one of the few naturally-formed pieces of water in the Beacons.

From here, follow the path for 2.5km down into Cwm Llwch and its parking and camping area, beyond which a lane leads in 800m to a crossroads. Turn right and follow the twisting lane for 1.5km back to the entrance to Cwm Gwdi car park.

◀ Looking towards Corn Du from Cwm Llwch

Cribyn

Distance 9km **Time** 3 hours 15
Terrain high open hillside and a broad ridge, with a steep and exposed final section; total height gain 550m
Map OS Explorer OL12 **Access** no public transport to the start

If you want a shorter outing in the Central Beacons, this climb up the distinctive pointy peak of Cribyn has a challenging approach ridge but a gentler return.

At the risk of punching above its weight, or perhaps height, there are some who compare this delightful peak to the giant craggy tooth of the Matterhorn that towers above the Swiss town of Zermatt. It certainly has some affinity of shape when viewed from the right angle and for those with little head for heights its final slope is certainly steep enough to give an alarming sense of exposure. But perhaps the true rival for the title of the 'Welsh Matterhorn' is the hill of Cnicht in Snowdonia in North Wales.

Start from Pont y Caniedydd where there is room for a few cars to park (GR039243). If parking here is unavailable, use the car park in Cwm Gwdi (GR025248) and follow the initial 2.5km of the Beacons Northern Horseshoe route.

**Cross the 'Bridge of the Singer' over the Nant Sere and follow the narrow lane steeply uphill, past Bailea and the entrance to Cwmcynwyn Farm. Here, the tarmac gives out and the lane becomes a

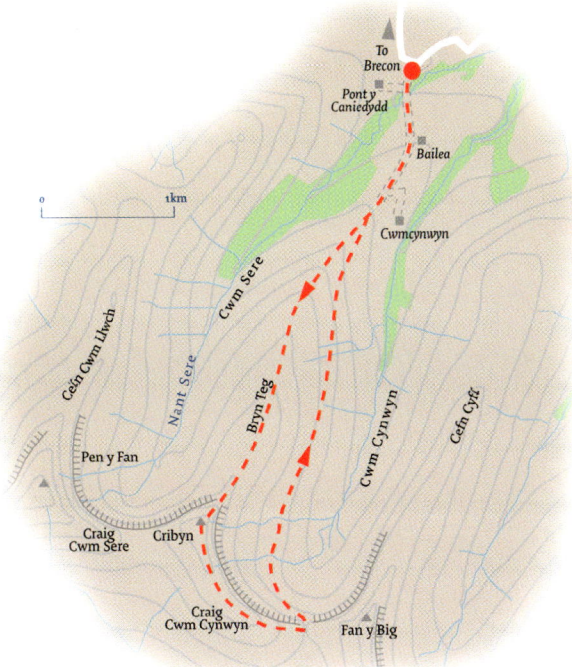

rough track which in 250m leads up to a gate and the open hillside.

Ahead is the long 2.5km climb up the ridge of Bryn Teg (Fair Hill) with a number of false tops up to the summit of Cribyn (795m). The final ascent is steep and can be a little daunting to the uninitiated or in strong winds. Although it is the lowest of the three central peaks, this top in some ways gives the most impressive views and it's a good point to trace in the northern cliffs of Pen y Fan the bands of sandstone which make up these hills.

To continue, descend south and eastwards around the rim of Cwm Cynwyn and then a little steeply down grassy slopes to the gap of Bwlch ar y Fan, with the slopes of Fan y Big across the other side – if time or inclination allows it's a simple ascent to this top. However, the circular route now bears left at the pass and follows the rough track northwards for just over 3km back to the gate at the edge of the open hillside. From here, retrace steps downhill to Pont y Caniedydd.

◀ Cribyn from Cefn Cwm Llwch

Beacons Northern Horseshoe

Distance 15km **Time** 5 hours 30
Terrain high mountain route with steep, exposed sections; total height gain 900m
Map OS Explorer OL12 **Access** no public transport to the start

A classic and rightly popular round of the peaks of the Central Beacons, taking in the three summits of Cribyn, Pen y Fan and Corn Du.

Start from the car park in Cwm Gwdi (GR025248). Walk back down to the road and take the right turn along the lane which wends its way eastwards. After 700m, at a sharp left bend, take the bridleway off right along the track to Plas-y-gaer ('Mansion of the Fort'). The path now passes to the left of the renovated buildings and then into fields. Here, leave the bridleway and follow the path which bears right to the corner of the first field beyond the buildings, and then along a fenceline before descending past the ruined Pant (which means 'hollow' and that's where it is) to the farm track to Old Crofftau ('House of Little Fields'). Bear left down to the road, where a right turn takes you across Pont y Caniedydd, the 'Bridge of the Singer', over the Nant Sere. Follow the narrow lane uphill, past Bailea and the entrance to Cwmcynwyn Farm, where the way becomes a rough track up to a gate and the open hillside.

Ahead is the long 2.5km climb up Bryn Teg (Fair Hill) to the summit of Cribyn (795m), whose final rise is steep. From Cribyn, descend westwards to the dip at the head of Cwm Sere, where there now

BEACONS NORTHERN HORSESHOE

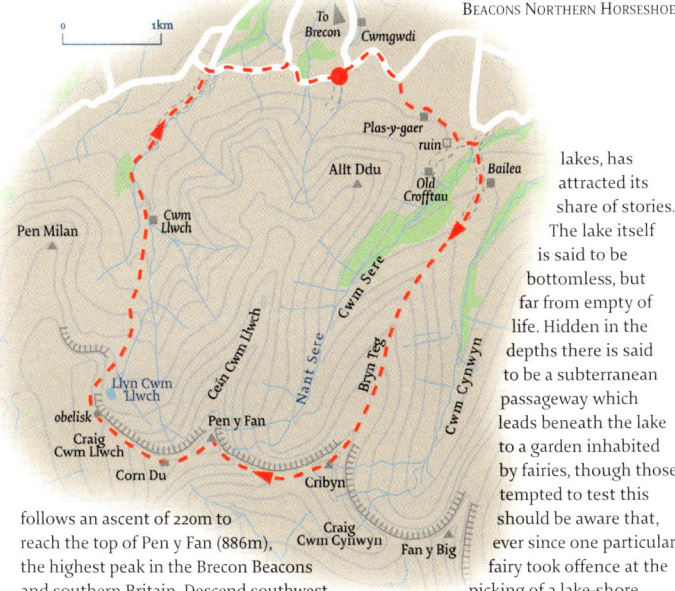

follows an ascent of 220m to reach the top of Pen y Fan (886m), the highest peak in the Brecon Beacons and southern Britain. Descend southwest around the rim of Cwm Llwch for a much shorter ascent up to the third peak, Corn Du (873m).

To leave the top of Corn Du, care should be taken, especially in poor visibility, to head northwest down Craig Cwm Llwch (rather than NNW where there is no descent route but, owing to people peering over the cliffs, there appears to be the start of one). Follow the path that keeps to the rim of the cwm and, once past the old memorial stone to the young boy Tommy Jones, keep descending to the right to Llyn Cwm Llwch, one of the few naturally formed pieces of water in the Beacons.

Llyn Cwm Llwch, like many mountain lakes, has attracted its share of stories. The lake itself is said to be bottomless, but far from empty of life. Hidden in the depths there is said to be a subterranean passageway which leads beneath the lake to a garden inhabited by fairies, though those tempted to test this should be aware that, ever since one particular fairy took offence at the picking of a lake-shore flower, the entrance has been closed to mortals. And if that is not warning enough, the waters hide a terrible giant who has threatened to flood the town of Brecon should anyone interfere with the lake. However, the crescent-shaped moraine of the cwm's retreating glacier has provided a solid enough dam for the town to be safe for the rest of this inter-glacial period.

From the lake, follow the path for 2.5km down into Cwm Llwch and its parking and camping area, beyond which a lane leads in 800m to a crossroads. Turn right and follow the twisting lane for 1.5km back to the entrance to Cwm Gwdi car park.

◀ The peaks of the Central Beacons from the north

Fan y Big

Distance 16km **Time** 5 hours
Terrain lanes, fields and high open hillside, with an ascent of 630m and a steep narrow final section up Fan y Big
Map OS Explorer OL12 **Access** bus to Llanfrynach from Brecon and Abergavenny

This is a jewel of a peak and the route starts from a pretty village with streams and woods – you couldn't ask for more from a day in the hills.

Start 5km southeast of Brecon in the pretty village of Llanfrynach, with its houses clustered around the church (GR074257). Take the lane at the northern end of the village, signed for Cantref. After 250m, at a bend, bear left into fields, soon passing an old weir and leats beside the pretty Nant Menasgin, with the site of a former Roman villa away to the right at Maesderwen.

Formal excavations have revealed what is more properly a complex rather than a simple country retreat at Maesderwen. There was also a substantial bathhouse with a series of rooms for hot and cold baths, a pattern well-attested from many other Roman sites. The villa is within easy reach of Brecon, where there was a military garrison of 500 men stationed.

After 1km, at a gate, cross a small side-stream and turn immediately right

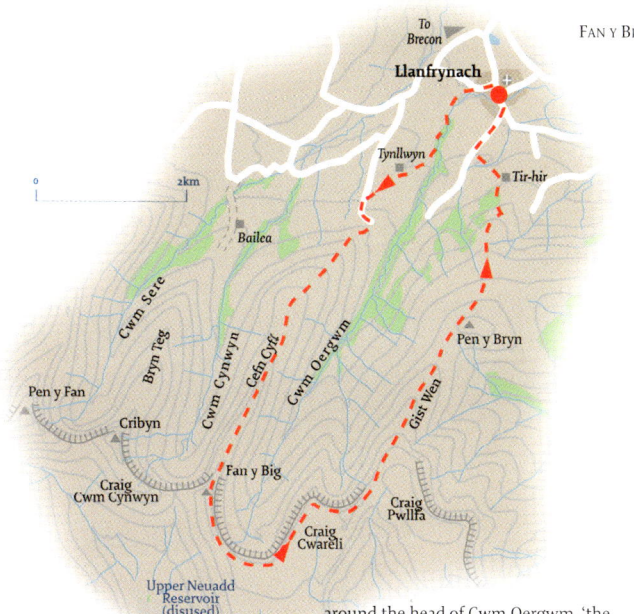

with the bridleway up to Tynllwyn. Now leave the bridleway and follow the field path signed 'To the Hill' across a lane and fields to a gate onto a second lane. Here, turn left up the lane for 350m to an old crossways.

Now, turn right (signed for Fan y Big) through a gateway up an old sunken lane to soon reach the open hillside. From here, the broad ridge of Cefn Cyff climbs in a southwesterly direction for 3.75km to the top of Fan y Big (719m), narrowing and steepening on the final approach, with great views west to the main peaks of the Beacons.

To continue, descend south and circle around the head of Cwm Oergwm, 'the Cold Valley', and then northwards to the craggy rim of Cwm Cwareli. Now the route descends the hill's broad northeast ridge of Gist Wen for 3.5km, passing below the lump of Pen y Bryn and across a stream above woodland. Once past the woods, bear left down the steepening bracken slope to a gate and stile above the wood of Coed Cae rebol. Follow the path as it drops steeply down through deciduous woodland for 250m, and bear right over a stile towards the impressive former farmhouse of Tir-hir. Here, turn left down a tarmac track to a lane, where a right turn leads in 700m to a T-junction on the outskirts of Llanfrynach. Now turn left to return to the centre of the village.

◀ Looking west from Fan y Big

Beacons Southern Horseshoe

Distance 11km **Time** 4 hours
Terrain high moorland paths over open hillside with some steep sections; total height gain 610m **Map** OS Explorer OL12
Access no public transport to the start

Another classic round of the three central peaks of Corn Du, Pen y Fan and Cribyn above the high former reservoirs, but very different in feel to the northern counterpart.

Start from the southern end of the decommissioned Neuadd Reservoirs where there is parking for a few cars (GR032179). If full, Neuadd car park has plenty of space, though it's 1.1km back down the road (GR037170).

Neuadd means 'hall' and is taken either to refer to the memory of a former building which was flooded by the construction in the late 18th century of these water sources for the valleys to the south, or as a metaphorical reference to the natural cirque of hills that surrounds them. A Bronze Age cairn and possible evidence of a crannog, a man-made island, were found in the upper reservoir, while in the valley below there are the remains of a small settlement. At a height of more than 450m, it makes for bleak living, whatever the age.

By 2021, the reservoirs had been fully drained and decommissioned by Welsh Water, with new trails and a footbridge built at Lower Neuadd Reservoir.

At the southern end of this former reservoir, cross the footbridge and take the winding gravel path onto the open slopes beyond, where an ascent of just over 200m on a boggy path brings you up onto the escarpment. Bear right and follow the cliff-edge path northwards along Graig Fan Ddu for 3.5km, beyond which the route narrows over Rhiw yr Ysgyfarnog (possibly 'Hillside of the Hare') and eventually descends to the dip of Bwlch Duwynt,

BEACONS SOUTHERN HORSESHOE

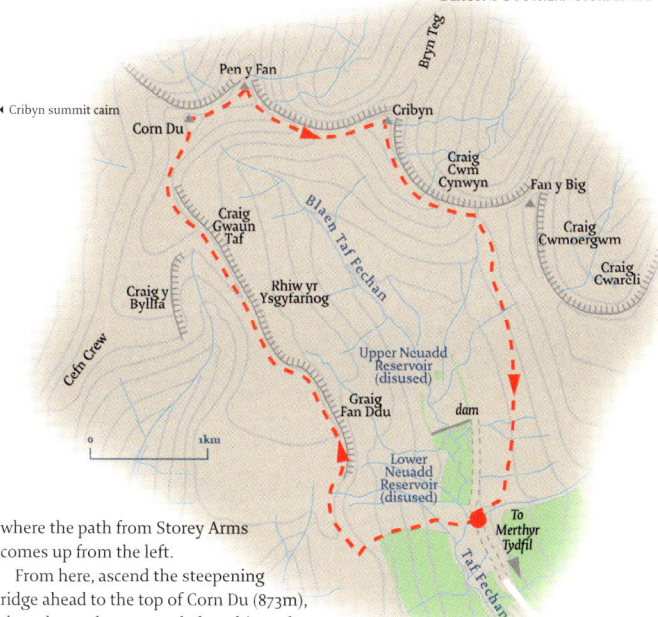

◀ Cribyn summit cairn

where the path from **Storey Arms** comes up from the left.

From here, ascend the steepening ridge ahead to the top of Corn Du (873m), though a path contours below this peak. To continue from the top, a short descent ENE takes you across a dip, beyond which the path circles the edge of Cwm Llwch up to Pen y Fan (886m), the highest peak in the Brecon Beacons and in southern Britain.

The descent off Pen y Fan in poor visibility can be a little confusing. The general direction is SSE, though a compass bearing is advisable if in doubt, and the path soon starts to circle eastwards above Craig Cwm Sere down to the low point at 665m, where there is a small patch of water. From here, it is a steep pull ENE up to the top of Cribyn, though this peak, too, can be bypassed on a path that contours below the top. To continue from the top of Cribyn (795m), descend south and eastwards around the rim of Cwm Cynwyn and then a little more steeply down grassy slopes to the gap of Bwlch ar y Fan.

Now turn right and descend the rough track southwards for 2.5km with long views down the Taff Valley. When almost level with the southern end of the lower reservoir, bear right onto a track which descends alongside a stream set down in a small gully and leads back in 250m to the buildings beside the former reservoir.

Talybont and Waun Rydd

Distance 17km **Time** 5 hours
Terrain old railway line, steep open hillside and high moorland; total height gain 600m **Map** OS Explorer OL12
Access bus to Talybont-on-Usk, 3km from the north end of Talybont Reservoir along the Taff Trail

Set out along a disused railway line before taking in the delights of waterfalls and open moorland slopes high above Talybont Reservoir.

Start from the north end of Talybont Reservoir where there is some limited parking (GR103205). Cross the dam to the reservoir's eastern side and turn right onto the Taff Trail, which follows the line of the old Brecon to Merthyr Junction Railway.

In 1860, work started to construct a railway from Brecon to Merthyr Tydfil to open up a route both for raw materials and goods from the coalfields of South Wales and also for daytrippers to admire the waterfalls and views of the Central Beacons. The Brecon and Merthyr Junction Railway was a mammoth undertaking, requiring not only an 11km ascent from Talybont to the head of Glyn Collwn, but also the boring of the country's highest railway tunnel through the mountainside of Torpantau.

Follow this trail for 7.5km through a mixture of woodland with occasional clearings and views above the eastern edge of the reservoir, passing the northern entrance to the old Torpantau Tunnel on the left of the track a little before the end of the forestry. The intrepid still venture along the 600m curving tunnel, though it's difficult to keep your feet dry as a stream now flows along its floor and the cutting at the southern entrance, near the site of

TALYBONT AND WAUN RYDD

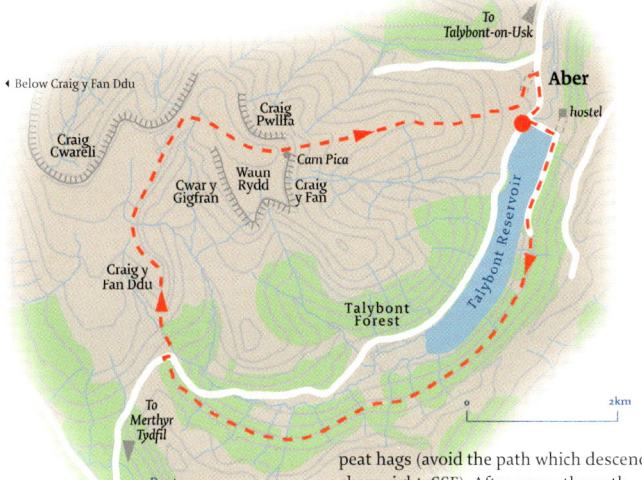

Torpantau Station, is flooded enough to require some wading.

At the mountain road, just beyond a gate and cattle grid, dogleg right for 100m along the road, then left and cross the Nant Bwrefwr just short of a car park.

Here, turn left (signed Beacons Way) past a series of waterfalls and ascend the steep southern slopes of Craig y Fan Ddu. From its high point, descend gently northwards, after 400m crossing above the cascade of Blaen Caerfanell, beyond which stone blocks take you NNE off the Beacons Way and across a boggy section. Now continue along Graig Fan Las for 1.5km to reach a low point at the edge of the escarpment above Cwm Cwareli.

Here, turn right (ESE) away from the escarpment along a grassy path through peat hags (avoid the path which descends sharp right, SSE). After 250m, the path bends a little to the right and starts to climb gently, passing two peaty pools on its way over the high moorland of Waun Rydd (769m) to the giant conical stone marker of Carn Pica (in mist, careful navigation with map and compass can be required on this section).

Now descend eastwards, steeply at first, for 2.5km over the rounded lump of Twyn Du and down through the bracken to a stile at the limit of Access Land. Beyond, the path drops into a tree-lined dell and crosses to the right side of the stream. In another 250m, ignore a path off right (signed Talybont Reservoir) and keep ahead on the old byway towards Aber, which soon bends to the left and reaches a lane. Go down the lane to the Talybont road and turn right for 700m to return to the reservoir.

Pant y Creigiau

Distance 8.5km **Time** 2 hours 30 **Terrain** forestry tracks and high moorland; total height gain 240m **Map** OS Explorer OL12 **Access** no public transport to the start

A short walk of contrasts – from forestry tracks to high moorland before returning through wooded Cwm Callan.

Start from the lay-by at the northern end of Pontsticill Reservoir (GR055143). By the mid-19th century, Merthyr Tydfil had become a booming industrial town of almost 50,000 inhabitants, drawn by the work in the coalmines and ironworks. The consequences for health and sanitary conditions were dire. In 1848 an outbreak of cholera killed more than 1500 people and a campaign followed, demanding the improvement of living and working conditions. The outcome was the building a decade later of Pentwyn Reservoir (also known locally as Dolygaer Lake), which was completed in 1858 to provide clean drinking water for the workers. The embankment of Pontsticill Reservoir (also known as Taf Fechan Reservoir) was completed in 1927 to incorporate the older reservoir in an enlarged scheme.

Walk across the head of the reservoir and, in 250m, turn left under a bridge carrying the Brecon Mountain Railway. Almost immediately turn left up through a gate and climb up above the railway to a wide forestry track. Bear left and follow this track northwards for 2km to the road. Here, bear right up the road for 500m to the top of the rise and then turn right again onto the clear path that climbs up

Pant y Creigiau

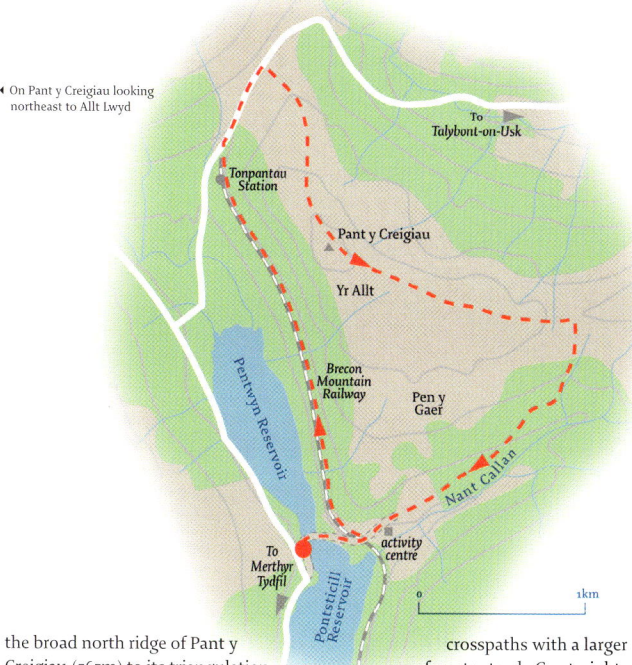

◀ On Pant y Creigiau looking northeast to Allt Lwyd

the broad north ridge of Pant y Creigiau (565m) to its triangulation point. To continue, follow the broad grassy ridge ESE for 1.5km over a slightly lower top and down to the prominent low point (GR070157). Now bear southeast off the ridge onto a smaller path which circles gradually down to the right to a forestry gate and track at the head of Cwm Callan after 400m.

Follow this track southwestwards, down through the plantation, crossing a stream after 350m. The track now levels out and in 200m reaches a slanted crosspaths with a larger forestry track. Go straight across and start to descend once more between old drystone walls and past the now ruined farmhouse of Blaencallan, still surrounded by deciduous woodland despite the encroaching conifers.

Continue down the track for another 500m to a gate, beyond which the road leads down past Parkwood Dolygaer Outdoor Centre and under the Mountain Railway bridge. From here, retrace the outward route across the reservoir.

9 THE CENTRAL BEACONS

Pontsticill and the Ystrad Stone

Distance 10km **Time** 3 hours
Terrain forestry tracks and high moorland; total height gain 270m
Map OS Explorer OL12 **Access** bus to Pontsticill (halfway along the route) from Merthyr Tydfil

Explore the valley above Pontsticill village before taking to the high moorland above the reservoir to reach an ancient Ogam-inscribed standing stone.

Start from the lay-by at the northern end of Pontsticill Reservoir (GR055143). Walk back along the road past the junction to Talybont and, in 50m, bear right onto a forestry track and the route of the Taff Trail. Follow this signed route for 3.5km as it weaves its way through the forestry on the reservoir's western slopes (after 1km take care to bear right at a track junction) to reach the road again near the reservoir's southern end. Here, bear right and walk down into Pontsticill village.

Just before the Red Cow Inn, turn left down the steep lane and across the bridge over the Taf Fechan. In another 50m, bear left up across the road and take the bridleway opposite (signed for Talybont), which climbs northeastwards above the reservoir for 750m, passing under the Brecon Mountain Railway and up through sheep enclosures to reach a gate set in a drystone wall.

From here, bear slightly right up over the open hillside for 200m to a broad track. Turn left and follow the track as it contours northwards and descends gently into Cwm Criban. To find the Ystrad Stone (463m), continue from the low point along the path for another 250m (GR073132). The stone, standing just under 1m high, is 20m to the left of the path.

PONTSTICILL AND THE YSTRAD STONE

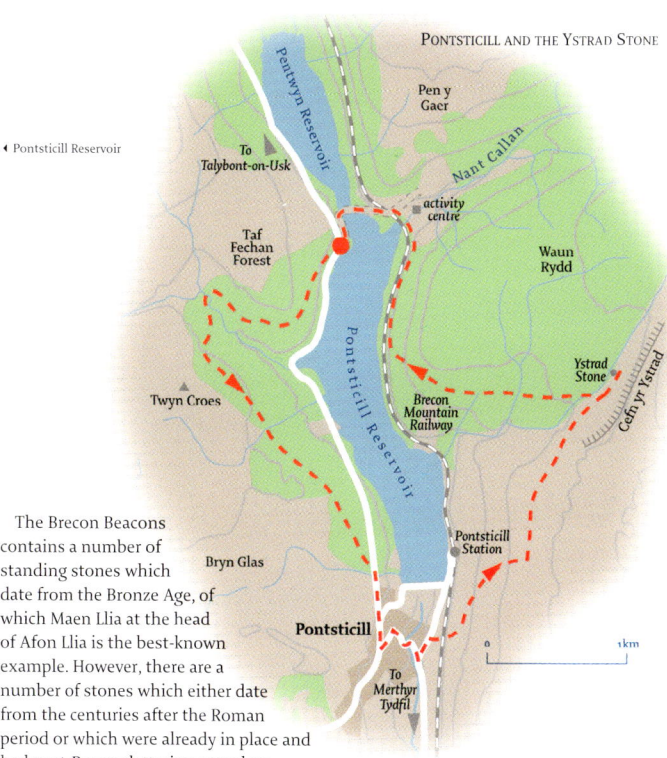

◀ Pontsticill Reservoir

The Brecon Beacons contains a number of standing stones which date from the Bronze Age, of which Maen Llia at the head of Afon Llia is the best-known example. However, there are a number of stones which either date from the centuries after the Roman period or which were already in place and had post-Roman lettering carved on them. The Ystrad Stone is inscribed with Ogam letters, though the marks and their meaning are faded. Ogam was a Celtic alphabet and its characters were written as a series of linear strokes at various angles. Other better-preserved examples can be seen in Y Gaer in Brecon.

From here, head westwards over rougher terrain for 800m towards a stand of forestry – to avoid tussocky ground, circle round to the right of the dip ahead, picking up a grassy quad-bike track to a stream, from where a path leads to, and passes above, the forestry. In another 400m, just beyond a gap in the forestry, bear left down through a plantation and under the Mountain Railway once more. Here, turn right onto a path beside the railway for 1.1km to reach the road by a railway bridge, where a left turn will take you across the head of the reservoir and back to the start.

The cliffs of Craig Cerrig-gleisiad ▶

In origin this 'Great Forest', lying to the west of the central peaks between the A470 and the A4067, was part of a royal hunting ground rather than a forest in the modern sense. In more recent times it has been heavily stocked with sheep, which in large part has given rise to the characteristic covering of grassy slopes, in places cropped short by centuries of grazing, but making for easier walking than the bracken and heather to the east. The area has also lent its name to the designation of the western half of the Beacons as a UNESCO Global Geopark, in recognition of its geological importance. The peaks here are not as high as those in the Central Beacons, but there is a greater sense of space and remoteness, while to the south the series of river gorges below Ystradfellte has become known for its substantial and numerous waterfalls.

Fforest Fawr

1. **Mynydd Illtud** — 68
   Delightful easy walking on this former common with great views

2. **Fan Frynych** — 70
   Enjoy a stroll along the ancient route of Sarn Helen before tackling steeper ground

3. **Craig Cerrig-gleisiad and Fan Fawr** — 72
   A contrasting walk of high moorland and valley trail, with a nature reserve to explore too

4. **Source of the Senni** — 74
   There's plenty to see on this route to the peak at the head of the Afon Senni

5. **Fan Gyhirych** — 76
   The promise of grand views from the top will spur you on around this hulk of a hill

6. **Fan Nedd and Maen Llia** — 78
   This route gives a short bracing walk on a blowy day or an excuse just to take things slowly

7. **Fan Llia and Fan Fawr** — 80
   Get off the beaten track over these largely pathless and remote hills

8. **Pontneddfechan waterfalls** — 82
   There's a waterfall around every corner – you even have to walk behind one on this route

Mynydd Illtud

Distance 11km **Time** 3 hours
Terrain paths and tracks over open moorland; total height gain 190m
Map OS Explorer OL12 **Access** bus to Libanus from Brecon starts on the A470, 2km from the start

Stroll around the perimeter of this exquisite former common – with its hillfort and fine views, it makes a great outing for youngsters.

Legend has it that St Illtud established a monastery close to Llanilltyd Farm in the 6th century and that he was buried here, though his remains are yet to be discovered. During his life he was associated with a number of miracles and extraordinary happenings. One story attempts to explain the origins of two separate standing stones found on the Mynydd Illtud and tells how the saint thwarted two robbers who repeatedly tried to steal some pigs. At the first attempt they drove the animals all night through the woods, but found themselves back where they started; the second time they headed for the mountains, but with the same result, whereupon Illtud turned them into stone. However, a rival explanation locates the stones to the southeast of Brecon near Llanhamlach at the site of Ty Illtud.

Start at the National Park Visitor Centre near Libanus, south of Brecon (GR977262). Go through the gate at the far end of the car park and take the bridleway northeastwards over the open hillside of the Mynydd Illtud. In 100m, where the path forks, bear right and follow the grassy track for 1km, passing straight over a crossways, to reach the single-track road along the broad ridge. Cross this and

◀ Looking west to Cefn Llechid from Allt Lom

descend over an unfenced road and a dip to the slope that leads up to the prominent hillfort of Twyn y Gaer (367m) with its panoramic views.

From here, retrace your steps across the dip and unfenced road but, before you reach the road along the ridge, bear right with the fence and follow the track along the northern edge of the open hillside. On reaching the road again, turn right for 500m to the point where you can bear right along a track for 750m to the high point of the Allt Lom, below which is an old quarry. Circle south again on the track on the other (western) side of this peninsula of open land. Once back at the road, bear right for 500m to the point where there is a large marshy pool on the left. Away to the right is the steep mound of a Norman motte, which can be reached by an out-and-back detour down the road for 200m and then along a path heading right across a field.

To continue from the marshy pool, take the track which weaves southeastwards for 1.4km across the open area of Traeth Mawr to reach a trackway on the southern edge of the Mynydd Illtud. Here, turn left and in a further 1km reach the approach road to the visitor centre.

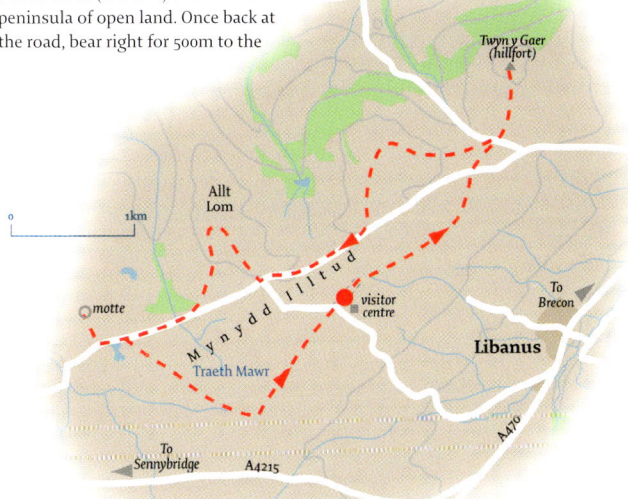

Fan Frynych

Distance 13.5km **Time** 4 hours
Terrain moorland tracks and paths and steep grassy slopes on Fan Frynych; total height gain 340m **Map** OS Explorer OL12
Access bus to Libanus from Brecon stops on the A470, 2km from the start

Pass along an old drovers' route into the brooding recess of Cwm Du before a return along an airy ridge, with great views to the central peaks of the Beacons.

On a gloomy overcast day, Cwm Du rightly earns its name of the 'Black Bowl'. It now forms part of a National Nature Reserve along with its neighbour Craig Cerrig-gleisiad on the eastern side of Fan Frynych. Both cwms are full of glacial features, and the steep cliffs and moraines are testament to this. However, the alignment of Cwm Du is rather unusual for a glaciated cwm. It hangs more than 100m above the Senni Valley and faces westwards and so is exposed to warmer winds. This would account for the relatively small extent of glaciation here. In addition, it is thought that the valley floor was once filled by a small lake, formed by a moraine dam located near the current bridge over the stream on the track of Sarn Helen.

From the National Park Visitor Centre near Libanus, south of Brecon (GR977262), walk back down the approach drive. Cross over the road onto the track and head southwestwards for 1.5km along the edge of the Mynydd Illtud. At the road, the A4215, cross over and follow the tarmac lane ahead for 850m with good views west to the Carmarthen Hills. Where the lane **bends right to the entrance to Forest**

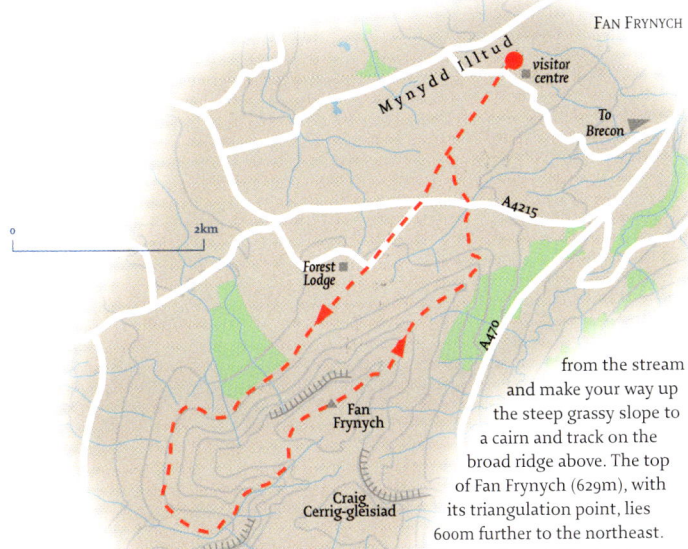

Lodge, continue ahead onto a track which passes below the northern slopes of Fan Frynych, before rounding the hill's northwest shoulder, where there are good views into the heart of Fforest Fawr.

Here, the track of Sarn Helen descends to Cwm Du, which is reached 4km after Forest Lodge. Where the track turns sharp right before a bridge over the Nant Cwm-du, bear left into Craig Cerrig-gleisiad National Nature Reserve.

From here, follow the path through the reserve as it heads up into the cwm itself. Cross the stream, after which the path narrows and starts to climb, and 100m beyond the second footbridge look out for a marker post. Here, turn left away from the stream and make your way up the steep grassy slope to a cairn and track on the broad ridge above. The top of Fan Frynych (629m), with its triangulation point, lies 600m further to the northeast. Now continue in the same direction on a track which descends the hill's northeast ridge, with great views right to the central peaks of the Beacons and ahead to the Black Mountains. In 1.2km where the track bears sharp left, ignore this turn and carry straight on through a gate on a grassy path over a small rise and down to a track junction and fence.

At the junction, dogleg left, then almost immediately right onto a narrow path down into a field, whose right-hand fenceline leads in 500m across a stream to a road, the A4215. Cross the road and follow the signed path over five fields, heading NNW, to reach the track on the southern edge of the Mynydd Illtud. Here, turn right to return to the National Park Visitor Centre.

◀ Descending the north ridge of Fan Frynych

Craig Cerrig-gleisiad and Fan Fawr

Distance 8km **Time** 3 hours **Terrain** open moorland and steep grassy slopes; total height gain 440m **Map** OS Explorer OL12 **Access** bus to Glyn Tarell from Brecon stops opposite Storey Arms on the route

One of the finest half-day walks in the Beacons – choose a clear day to appreciate the best the route has to offer.

The Taff Trail is a long-distance walking and cycling route linking Cardiff to Brecon. For 90km, it follows the course of the River Taff, along canal towpaths and disused railways, and passes through the town of Merthyr Tydfil, famous as the 19th-century 'iron capital' of South Wales. From here, there are two branches to the route as it crosses into the Brecon Beacons National Park. The eastern one heads into the hills over the high pass of Torpantau before descending past Talybont and on towards Brecon. The western route shadows the line of the main A470 and it is part of this section that this route follows.

Start from the lay-by and small picnic area, 4km south of Libanus on the A470 midway between Brecon and Merthyr Tydfil (GR971222). Take the path on the right of the stream up into the cwm. Cross a stone wall and, in 50m, bear left across the stream to climb the east shoulder of Craig Cerrig-gleisiad (steep in places) to a kink in the fence at a height of 620m.

Cross the fence and descend southwards for 1.5km across grassy moorland on an intermittent path which snakes around a few peat hags and, lower down, some boggy sections. In clear weather, the expansiveness and remoteness of this section is impressive, if a little eerie, though in poor visibility a

◂ The northern slopes of Fan Fawr

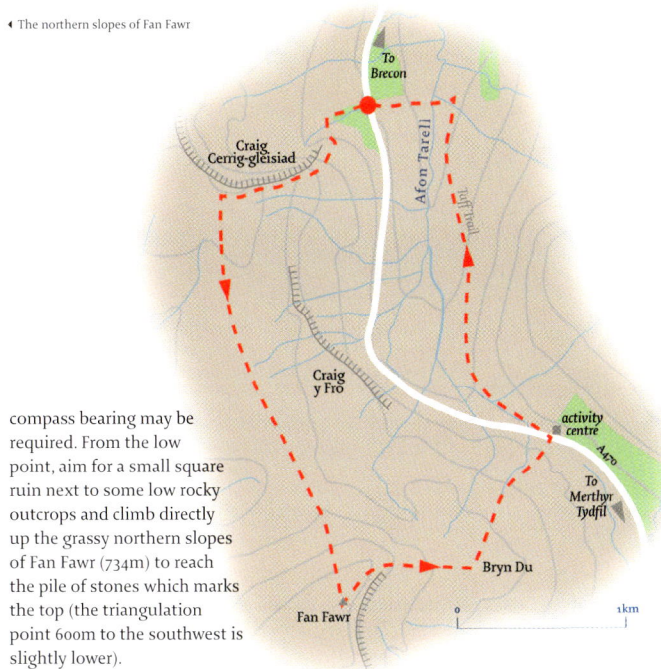

compass bearing may be required. From the low point, aim for a small square ruin next to some low rocky outcrops and climb directly up the grassy northern slopes of Fan Fawr (734m) to reach the pile of stones which marks the top (the triangulation point 600m to the southwest is slightly lower).

To descend, follow the hill's northeast shoulder which, after the initial grassy slope, is a little steep. Below this section, at a height of 580m, bear left (avoid the faint path which continues over Bryn Du) across a more level boggy section before the final descent to Storey Arms Outdoor Education Centre on the A470.

Cross the road and turn left onto the Taff Trail on a broad track which descends gently northwards above the tree-dotted Afon Tarell. After 2km, once opposite the cliffs of Craig Cerrig-gleisiad once more, look out for a permissive path which descends sharp left down a field to a footbridge across the Tarell. Now a final bit of puff is required to climb directly up the slope on the opposite side to the A470 again, a short distance south of the start.

Source of the Senni

Distance 23km **Time** 7 hours
Terrain tracks and paths over remote high moorland; total height gain 750m
Map OS Explorer OL12 **Access** bus to Defynnog from Sennybridge and Brecon

Explore the upper reaches of the Senni Valley, saved a generation ago from being flooded beneath a reservoir, and enjoy some of the finest views the area has to offer.

Start from the village of Defynnog, south of Sennybridge (GR925277). Approaching the walk, you may well see the red-bordered signs for the army's Sennybridge Training Area – SENTA is the military's typical use of acronym – and you're likely to hear the sound of weapons being fired off to the north on the Mynydd Epynt, as the ranges are in use most days of the year. The training area lies outside, though right next to, the boundary of the national park, but since the Army School of Infantry moved to Brecon some years ago the area has been even more heavily used to train the nation's troops.

Walk along the A4067 over the Afon Senni for 250m and take the first lane on the left, looking out for the footpath on the right into fields after 200m. Follow this delightful old trackway as it weaves an ascent southwards, passing just to the left of the hillfort of Twyn y Gaer. From here, the track descends in 1.1km to a lane, which leads in another 500m for Brychgoed Chapel with its Georgian Gothic windows. Continue up the lane, in 500m passing a house, and through a gate onto open hillside. Now follow the track by the fenceline on the right for 1.3km up to the road, where a right turn brings you in

300m to a house and a patch of forestry.

From here, the route turns left (SSE) to shadow the boundary wall and fence which heads up a broad grassy switchback ridge for 3.75km to Bwlch y Duwynt – you can pass over the unnamed top with a triangulation pillar at 603m (GR912216), and then bear southwest to rejoin the boundary wall as it heads to Bwlch y Duwynt. (To cross the boundary fence and wall, try either just above the house and forestry or 1km up the ridge, where there is a stile at the kink in the fenceline 300m north of the unnamed top.)

From Bwlch y Duwynt, drop left, crossing the source of the Senni, to a second, lower pass and climb the northwest ridge of Fan Nedd (663m) to a prominent cairn, which lies 450m north of the hill's high point. Descend from the cairn along the northeast ridge. Cross the road and head northeast for 700m over the moorland, initially by a wall, to pick up the clear track of Sarn Helen. (If you want to see the impressive standing stone of Maen Llia, detour south for 450m along the road before heading for Sarn Helen.)

Turn left along this high-level track for 2.3km to a bridge at the entrance to Cwm Du and then uphill for 1.2km to the point where Sarn Helen bends to the northeast. Here, bear left downhill to reach a lane which goes over a crossroads and then twists its way northwards past the house of Cefn Fedw Fawr to a T-junction (GR934252).

Turn left past Pantglas Farm and in another 250m, at a T-junction, dogleg right, then left to descend to the Afon Senni. Just beyond the bridge, turn right onto a hedged track. This leads past a stone house and barns, continuing between fields for 1.2km before reaching a lane which takes you back to Defynnog.

◂ High above the Senni Valley looking east

Fan Gyhirych

Distance 12km **Time** 3 hours 30
Terrain tracks and rough intermittent paths over open hillside; total height gain 380m **Map** OS Explorer OL12
Access no public transport to the start

A tough little circuit of an easily bypassed hill, ideal on a late summer's day to watch the sun set over the western peaks.

In the early part of the 19th century, the landscape of the Fforest Fawr was changed significantly. The Enclosure Act of 1815 led to the large-scale sale of land owned by the Crown, and farmers from other parts of Britain were encouraged to relocate and set up new ventures. Many Scottish sheep farmers were attracted by the opportunities in South Wales, not least the McTurk family. Two brothers, Robert and Thomas McTurk, settled at Cnewr in the 1850s and successfully introduced Cheviot sheep and Galloway cattle. Their descendants still run the Cnewr Estate, one of the largest of its type in Wales. Until another Act of Parliament, the Countryside and Rights of Way Act 2000, came into being there were only three permissive routes across these hills. Now people can wander where previously only sheep and cattle were allowed to go.

FAN GYHIRYCH

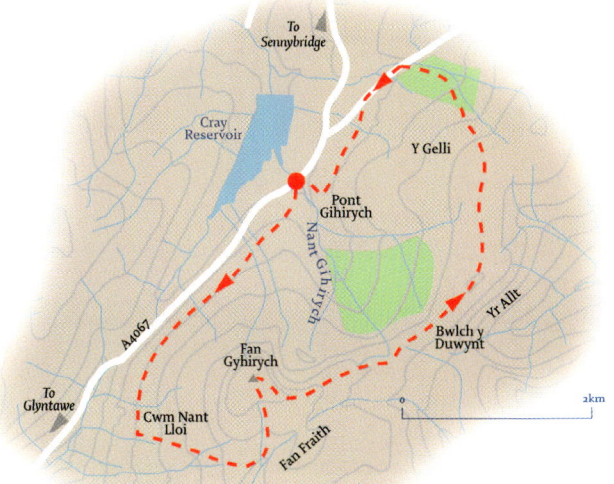

Start at the lay-by at Pont Gihirych Viaduct above Cray Reservoir, 8km south of Sennybridge on the A4067 (GR887211). Walk across the old viaduct and go left through the gate onto the open hillside. Climb the grassy slope up to the higher of the two dismantled tramways.

Bear right onto the line of this second tramway, which is boggy in places, and follow it as it contours around the northern slopes of Fan Gyhirych, rising slightly above Bwlch Bryn-rhudd (Pass of the Red Hill) opposite a reconstructed tower. Here, the tramway bears round to the south for 1km, narrowing to a path through Cwm Nant Lloi, to reach a stile over a fence.

Across the stile, leave the line of the tramway and follow the fenceline uphill for 1.1km over tussocky ground, past a small ruin and across a stream, up to a track which skirts the south side of the hill. Turn left onto the track for 500m to the right bend, before striking up the broad and pathless south ridge of Fan Gyhirych (725m) to its triangulation point, from which on a clear day there are views across the whole of the Brecon Beacons.

Now cross the plateau and descend the hill's east ridge, with steep slopes on the left, to rejoin the track over the broad Bwlch y Duwynt. Pass some livestock pens at the side of the track before descending northwards for 2.5km. Turn left down the road for 800m and, just before the A4067, bear left through a gateway onto the dismantled tramway once more. After 500m, head right, down the slope towards the viaduct and the lay-by.

◀ Fan Gyhirych

Fan Nedd and Maen Llia

Distance 8km **Time** 3 hours
Terrain remote and, in places, steep grassy slopes over open hillside with an ascent of 310m **Map** OS Explorer OL12
Access no public transport to the start

A short but remote route over the high ground above the area's most enigmatic standing stone.

Start from the car park at Blaen Llia, 3km north of the village of Ystradfellte (GR927164). Access to this point from the north is along a high and, at times, steep mountain road which could be problematic in wintry conditions.

Walk back up the car park's access track to the mountain road. Turn right and go along the road for 500m, passing the point where Sarn Helen, a Roman road which linked the forts at Brecon and Neath, heads southwest. Just beyond the end of the forestry plantation on the left is a stile. Cross the fence here onto what is now designated as Access Land. Here, you can also glimpse the thin pinnacle of Maen Llia above the horizon at the head of the valley.

To ascend, initially follow the edge of the plantation and the Nant y Groes (Stream of the Crossroads) – there is an intermittent path, but it is easily lost in the long tussocky grass. After 400m, bear away from the plantation and head northwest with the stream for a further

Fan Nedd and Maen Llia

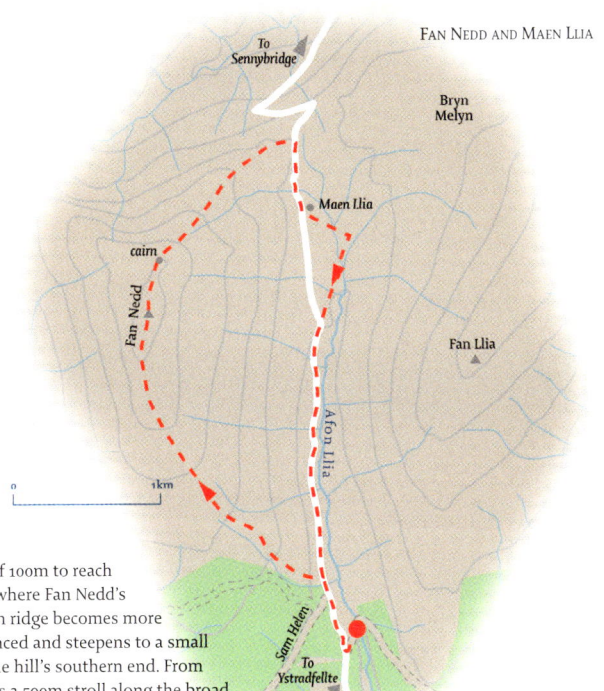

ascent of 100m to reach a point where Fan Nedd's southern ridge becomes more pronounced and steepens to a small top at the hill's southern end. From here, it is a 500m stroll along the broad ridge to the triangulation point marking the highest point of Fan Nedd (663m).

To descend, continue for 450m along the ridge to the prominent cairn at its northern end. From here, there is a choice of routes down to the Bronze Age standing stone of Maen Llia. Either descend in a direct line of sight down the hill's eastern slopes to the stone or, if a slightly gentler descent is required, or perhaps in mist, head down the hill's northeast ridge to reach the road 450m north of the standing stone. The stone is thought to have been a waymarker for those traversing this high pass at the head of the Nant Llia.

To continue from Maen Llia, go southeastwards over rough tussocky ground for 400m to where the track of Sarn Helen comes in from the left (or alternatively, if it's very wet, go down the road to the point where this track meets the road). From here, pick a way along the bubbling Afon Llia's right-hand bank until you reach the road. Carry on, with the Afon Llia on your left, all the way back to Blaen Llia.

◀ Maen Llia

7 FFOREST FAWR

Fan Llia and Fan Fawr

Distance 16km **Time** 3 hours 30
Terrain remote and, in places, steep grassy slopes, with a stream to ford; total height gain 770m **Map** OS Explorer OL12
Access no public transport to the start

Stride out over the sheep-cropped grass of these remote hills and enjoy the solitude and sense of space.

Start from the car park at Blaen Llia, 3km north of the village of Ystradfellte (GR927164). Access to this point from the north is along a high and, at times, steep mountain road which could be problematic in wintry conditions.

Cross the footbridge over the Afon Llia and bear left up to a stile and onto the open hillside beyond. Make a rising traverse NNE up onto the broad south ridge of Fan Llia (632m), where a path can be followed up to a cairn just before the hill's high point.

Continue along the ridge for a further 1km over the rise of Fan Dringarth to its northern end, where there is a landslip area on the right. Just beyond this, head right, off the ridge, and descend eastwards down grassy slopes, a little steeply at times but with no real difficulties, to the point where the Nant Mawr joins the main stream (GR950197).

Ford the stream and continue in an easterly direction for 2km straight up the grassy slopes ahead for an ascent of 325m to the top of Fan Fawr (734m). From here, go southwest past the hill's triangulation point, a little beyond which the path peters out, and continue down grassy slopes to the southern end of Ystradfellte Reservoir.

Fan Llia and Fan Fawr

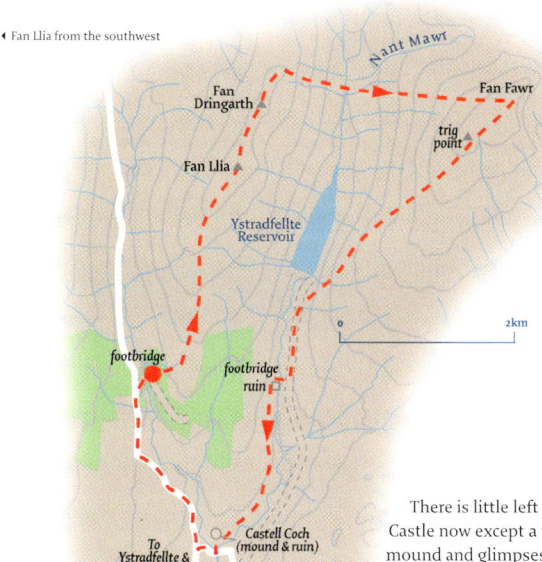

◀ Fan Llia from the southwest

Walk down the access road for 1.1km past some sheep pens and, 50m before a gate across the road, bear steeply right down to a footbridge across the Afon Dringarth. Bear left onto an old bridleway, up past a ruined house, and head left (SSW) for 1.4km over sheep pastures with forestry plantations away to the right. Now pick up a broad track, muddy at times, which descends southwards to Nantywenynen Farm, where a right turn leads down past the now-wooded mound of Castell Coch.

There is little left of the Red Castle now except a wooded mound and glimpses of earthworks and boulders of red sandstone, which perhaps accounts for the name. Originally there was a keep with a courtyard and some substantial walls. There are a number of theories about its history. It may have been a former hunting lodge of the Fforest Fawr, perhaps dating back as far as the 12th century. Another theory is that it was the site of the Fforest Court, where felons were tried and disputes over land and property were settled.

At the road, turn right for 200m to reach a T-junction and turn right again to follow the mountain road for 1.8km to arrive back at Blaen Llia car park.

Pontneddfechan waterfalls

Distance 15km **Time** 3 hours 30 (including detours) **Terrain** paths through woodland and fields, and over open hillside, boggy in places, with a crossing behind a waterfall; total height gain 320m
Map OS Explorer OL12 **Access** bus to Pontneddfechan from Neath

Wander from waterfall to waterfall on this rollercoaster of a route, past former industrial sites and through swathes of woodland once used as a source of charcoal.

In the middle of the 18th century, Pontneddfechan was a centre of industry. The Vale of Neath Powder Company located its Gunpowder Works here, attracted by the supplies of timber for charcoal and the volume of flowing water to power its machinery. Limestone was quarried from Craig y Ddinas and taken by horse-drawn tramway to Pont Walby Brickworks to the west of the village. Even the silica needed to make bricks to line the brickworks was sourced from here.

Start from the village, just off the A465 between Hirwaun and Glyn Neath. There is roadside parking near the Angel Inn (GR899075). Walk past the inn and look for a gate across the road from the back of the building, marked 'Bro'r Sgydau'. Beyond this, follow a broad level path for 1.5km to a footbridge over the Afon Pyrddin. To visit Sgwd Gwladus, detour left after the bridge for 300m. The onward route undulates for 1.8km to Pont Melin-fach, still along the west bank of the Afon Nedd Fechan, and past three more waterfalls.

At Pont Melin-fach, turn right over the bridge up the road for 500m to a bend where the gradient steepens. Here, look out for a permissive path off left (signed for Heol Fawr). Follow the waymarks up beside a stream and over a field to an old twisting byway, where a right turn soon

PONTNEDDFECHAN WATERFALLS

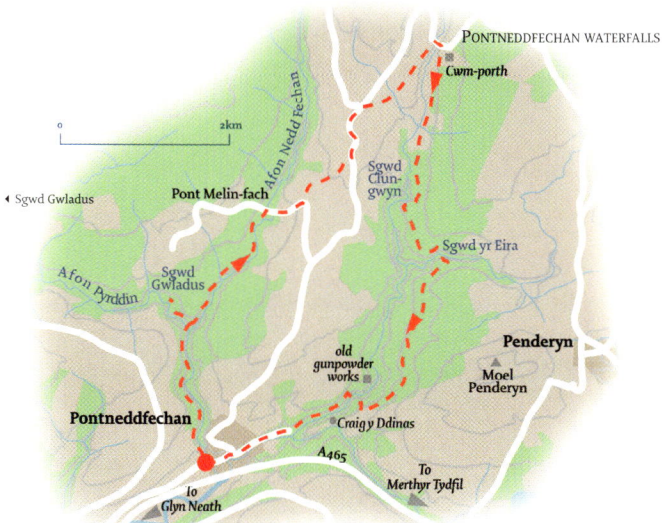

brings you to the farm of Heol Fawr. Beyond this, continue along the lane to a right bend after 150m. Here, turn left over fields in a northeasterly direction and through a small patch of woodland for 350m to the road, where a left turn takes you up past Bryn Bwch. At the top of the rise, take the bridleway on the right (signed for Porth yr Ogof) which descends gently for 1km (after 250m take care to bear left with the bridleway) to Cwm Porth, where there is a car park.

From Cwm Porth, take the yellow-signed footpath southwards, in 50m bearing left to 'Blue Pool and Waterfalls', and soon emerge on the east bank of the Afon Mellte. After 1.3km, pass a footbridge and climb up to the left above the river to Marker Post 13. Here, you can drop right to detour to Sgwd Clun-gwyn. To continue, follow the path (signed for Sgwd yr Eira) above the Afon Mellte for 1.2km through Marker Posts 16-35. Now bear steeply right down steps to Sgwd yr Eira. The onward route requires you to cross behind the waterfall on a broad shelf before climbing out of the far side of the gorge up more steep steps.

At the top, bear right (signed for Craig y Ddinas) along a path, boggy in places, through and alongside sections of forestry. After 1km, the path bears to the southwest and starts to descend more open hillside. At a path junction after another 1km (signed with a purple cannon marker), either continue straight on or bear sharp right to follow the Gunpowder Trail across a footbridge to the former Gunpowder Works, where the trail turns left. Both routes reach the quiet road which returns you to Pontneddfechan after 1km.

The westernmost area of the Beacons is known as the Black Mountain. Although it shares its name, albeit in singular form, with the easternmost part, the terrain is a complete contrast. The steep escarpment of Bannau Brycheiniog presents an imposing northern wall more than 800m in height, approached over miles of high open moorland. Here, too, are the headwaters of the River Usk, dammed to form a reservoir in the middle of the 20th century, and to the south the River Tawe gathers itself to flow towards the sea at Swansea, beyond which, on a clear day, it is possible to see the coastline of the Gower. Despite its relative remoteness, increasing numbers of walkers are venturing out into this part of the national park to sample its delights. There are waterfalls, caves, old quarries, raised bogs and one of the best ridge walks in the whole of southern Britain.

Looking west from the slopes of the Black Mountain ▸

The Black Mountain

1 Mynydd Myddfai 86
Moorland walking at its best –
and the route starts from the prettiest
of secluded villages

2 Bannau Brycheiniog horseshoe 88
A bold but pathless approach to this
classic round of the western peaks

**3 Fan Hir and the
Headwaters of the Tawe** 90
Perhaps the best ridge walk in the
Beacons and one of the loveliest
waterfalls too

4 Foel Fraith and Garreg Lwyd 92
Keep your map and compass handy
on this short walk over largely
pathless terrain

5 Tair Carn Uchaf 94
Pick a good day to find your way
over the challenging ground and
to make the best of the views

① The Black Mountain

Mynydd Myddfai

Distance 15km **Time** 4 hours 30
Terrain fields and remote moorland with pathless sections; total height gain 440m
Map OS Explorer OL12 **Access** no public transport to the start

Choose a clear day to experience the best this high moorland round of Usk Reservoir has to offer.

Start from the village of Cwmwysg, 3km southwest of Trecastle, where there is parking in a lay-by next to a postbox and footbridge over the River Usk (GR851283). Walk up the road past the chapel for 800m and turn right onto a permissive path which tracks northwards up past Pentwyn Farm, over fields and up to the right of a thin strip of forestry. Here, the path doglegs right for 150m and then left over two more fields up to the Roman road running along the top of the ridge.

Turn left along the road and in 200m pass a triangulation point on the right, beyond which the tarmac ends. Follow the track as it heads northwest over Mynydd-bach Trecastell where, after 2km, you can detour uphill right to see the Roman camp of Y Pigwn, whose defensive ditches are still visible. From here, continue along the track as it bears round to the southwest and climbs past old tilestone pits on the left. Cross the dip of Pen y Bylchau and follow the track up to the triangulation point at 440m, marking the top of the broad ridge of Mynydd Myddfai. Descend gently southwest for 1km (there are more tilestone quarries down to the left here) and, 100m beyond the low point, bear SSE off the ridge. Descend pathless grassy slopes for 1.3km, passing a prominent cairn after 500m, to the western tip of Usk Reservoir.

◂ Above Usk Reservoir looking south

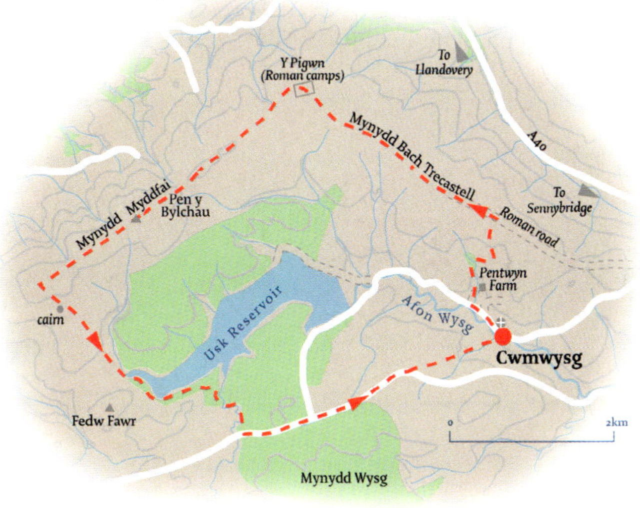

Whether the legend of the Lady of the Lake is true (see next walk), there is more historical credence to the story that her eldest son, Rhiwallon, founded a long line of physicians. After her return to the lake, his mother appeared to him at a place called Llidiad y Meddygon (the Gate of the Physicians), which is located at the western end of what is now Usk Reservoir, and taught him secret powers of healing with plants. In Myddfai Church, there is a stone listing the physicians, and a medieval medical treatise, found in the library of Jesus College, Oxford, was published in 1861 under the title *Meddygon Myddfai*.

Cross the fence by the ford and follow the track through woodland round the south side of the reservoir. In 1.5km, the track leads to a footbridge at the next inlet and then bears right up to the road in another 500m, emerging opposite Glasfynydd car park.

Here, turn left up the unfenced road for 2km to a sharp right bend. Continue for another 100m and, just past the high point and a small patch of forestry, turn left for 50m along a track. Now bear right along the right-hand edge of a small triangular patch of forestry to pick up the line of an old sunken way descending ENE for 700m to a gate onto a lane, which leads down to the houses of Cwmwysg and the footbridge across the river.

Bannau Brycheiniog horseshoe

Distance 12km **Time** 4 hours 30
Terrain a mountain route with exposed sections and some pathless terrain; total height gain 700m **Map** OS Explorer OL12
Access no public transport to the start

Gain a great sense of space on this classic round of the highest western peaks of the Beacons and watch out for the red kites from the Feeding Station at Llanddeusant.

Start from the parking area, 2.4km east of the small village of Llanddeusant. This is reached from the village by driving down the hill for 1.5km, bearing left at a junction along a track and past a farm. In another 300m, just before a second farm, turn right down over a cattle grid and follow the rough track for 200m to the parking area just before the bridge (GR799238).

Walk along the track over the bridge for 100m and at the bend strike off left up the pathless but easy-going grassy slopes of Twyn yr Esgair, heading southeast for 1.6km up the broad ridge, between the dips of the Nant Melyn to the left and the Nant Coch to the right. At a height of 600m, start to bear eastwards round the headwaters of the Nant Melyn and pick up a substantial sheep trod which contours around the northern flanks of Fan Foel to the hill's north ridge.

Here, ignore a path which climbs directly up the north ridge, but instead continue to contour, bearing southeast on a clear path which passes beneath the hill's gullied northeast slopes and, after

BANNAU BRYCHEINIOG HORSESHOE

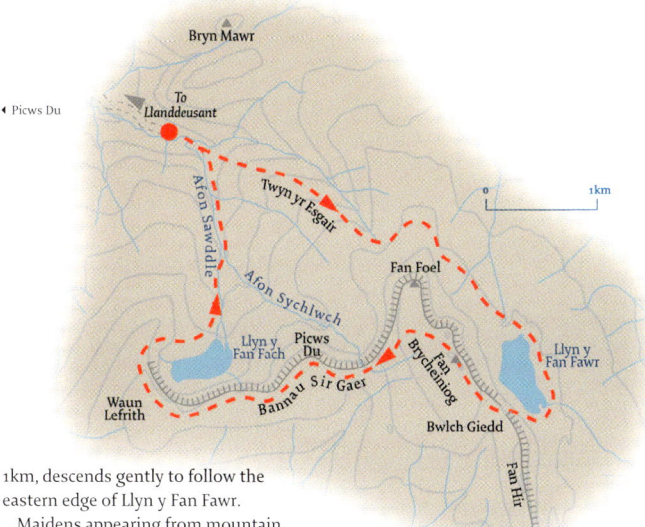

◀ Picws Du

1km, descends gently to follow the eastern edge of Llyn y Fan Fawr.

Maidens appearing from mountain lakes are the staple of many hill regions and this llyn has a famous one. It involves a shy young farmer from the northern foot of the mountain persuading the lady, who appears to him out of the lake, with an offer to share his bread. At the third attempt he is successful, but his love imposes the condition that, should he strike her three times, she will leave him. There follow over the years, in between child-bearing, a 'playful slap' for forgetfulness, a hand 'pressed on her shoulder' for lateness, and a blow to 'check her laughter' at a funeral. And so the woman gathers all her livestock, which she had brought as a dowry, and keeps her promise.

Cross the lake's outflow stream at its southern end and climb the clear path to Bwlch Giedd. From here, bear right and a short climb takes you to the top of Fan Brycheiniog (802m) and its triangulation point.

To continue, follow the escarpment edge north to Fan Foel and then SSW to descend to Bwlch Blaen-Twrch. From here, it's a steep pull up to Picws Du (749m), the highest point in Carmarthenshire. The route now lies westwards, still following the escarpment, to the lower top of Waun Lefrith. Here, bear right and follow the ridge round as it descends north and then east down to the dam and rescue shelter at the north end of Llyn y Fan Fach. Now descend the reservoir's access track for 2km past a series of weirs and some waterworks buildings back to the start.

Fan Hir and the Headwaters of the Tawe

Distance 15km **Time** 5 hours
Terrain a mountain route with exposed sections and some pathless terrain; total height gain 650m **Map** OS Explorer OL12
Access bus to Glyntawe from Swansea and Brecon

One of the finest ridge walks in the Beacons leads to the high top of Fan Brycheiniog before a return via the secluded Afon Haffes and its hidden cascade of the Black Waterfall.

Start at the Tafarn-y-Garreg pub on the A4067 at the northern edge of Glyntawe (GR848171). If you intend to visit the pub park in the overflow car park next to the pub. Take the Beacons Way on the other side of the road and cross the River Tawe over a footbridge. Bear right along the riverbank for 150m, then left through a gate to a stile by sheep pens just above Ty Henry farm.

Follow the path northwest as it ascends the open hillside for 4km, steeply at first and then across a more level, boggy area before climbing the well-defined upper section of Fan Hir's long south ridge. Descend to Bwlch Giedd, where a final pull takes you to the high point of Fan Brycheiniog (802m).

People walking along this long ridge often wonder at what appears to be a much smaller ridge running parallel to the main one at the base of the steep eastern scarp slope. This unusual feature has made many geologists scratch their heads too. Until the 1990s, it was thought that this feature was a pronival rampart, formed by rocks from the top of the ridge sliding down to the base over a bed of

Fan Hir and the Headwaters of the Tawe

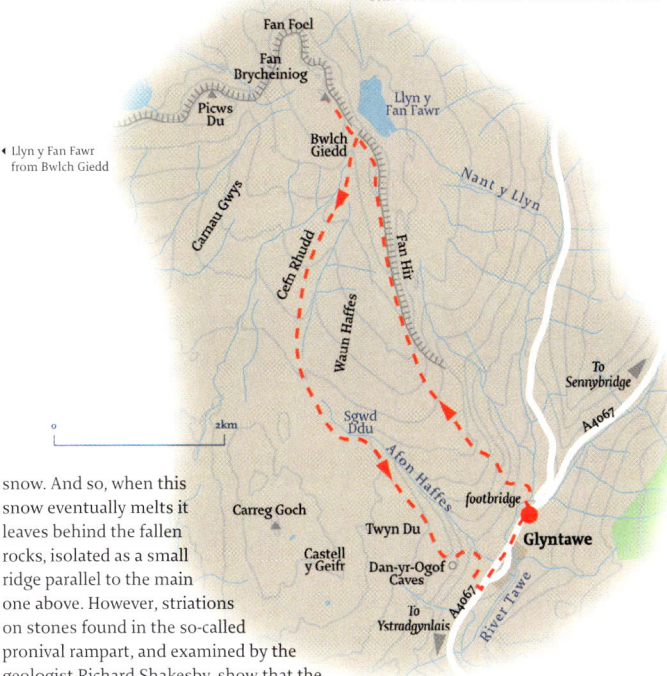

◀ Llyn y Fan Fawr from Bwlch Giedd

snow. And so, when this snow eventually melts it leaves behind the fallen rocks, isolated as a small ridge parallel to the main one above. However, striations on stones found in the so-called pronival rampart, and examined by the geologist Richard Shakesby, show that the feature must have been created by a small but active glacier and, therefore, is actually a moraine.

From the summit, retrace your steps down to Bwlch Giedd and, by a pile of stones, bear right on an intermittent path which descends southwards. After 500m bear slightly to the southwest down the grassy slopes of Cefn Rhudd for 2km, following a line above the infant Afon Haffes. Lower down, the path becomes more distinct. Continue to follow the grassy path as it turns southeast, over boggier ground, and then east to the impressive Sgwd Ddu ('Black Waterfall').

Contour southeast for 1km over pathless ground to Twyn Du. Here, descend in the same direction for another 300m to pick up a track which heads south, more steeply, down to a fence. Bear left (northeast) for 500m down the broad grassy track, past an old quarry, to some sheepfolds. Here, bear right on a path down to a campsite, where a track leads out to the A4067 on the southern edge of Glyntawe.

Foel Fraith and Garreg Lwyd

Distance 8km **Time** 2 hours 30
Terrain remote moorland with some pathless sections; total height gain 280m
Map OS Explorer OL12 **Access** no public transport to the start

A short but rather challenging outing over often pathless terrain which has all you would expect of a much longer day in the hills.

Wandering over these open hills, it is likely that overhead there will come into view the majestic sight of the fork-tailed red kite, soaring on the updrafts and as magnificent as any eagle. And it is quite possible to see more than one at a time wheeling in the sky – even four or five is not unusual nowadays. However, at the start of the 20th century the red kite was all but extinct and perhaps only a handful of pairs were actually breeding. The bird was considered by farmers and gamekeepers to be a serious pest in need of control. Now, in Wales, the Welsh Kite Trust believes there to be more than 2500 breeding pairs. In this part of the world, their fortunes have been reversed largely by the Red Kite Feeding Station, which lies a few miles away in the village of Llanddeusant.

Start from the car park and viewpoint on the A4069 below Herbert's Quarry (GR730192). Walk up the road for 100m and, just before a memorial stone, turn left onto a track and take this for 500m, skirting the northern edge of the former

Herbert's Quarry. Where the track ends, descend the now grassy slagheap and go east over pathless terrain for another 500m to pass above the waterfalls in the cleft of the infant Afon Clydach.

From here, head ENE up pathless but easy-going grassy slopes for 1.1km along outcroppings of limestone and past an old stone marker, now wedged upright, to the cairn that marks the rounded top of Cefn y Truman. Go east for 600m across a small dip to Cefn y Cylchau, whose moorland top is marked only by a small pile of stones. The route now turns south for 1.5km across the boggy low point of Blaen y Cylchau and straight up the grassy northern flanks of Foel Fraith (602m), whose exact top is tricky to locate among the peat hags.

Descend WSW, picking up a path after 200m down to the broad low point, where a path climbs for 1km up the eastern slopes of Garreg Lwyd (616m) and over its broad rock-strewn top to a large cairn and triangulation point.

Go northwest over the plateau for 300m, and then start to descend more steeply to hit the A4069 at a higher car park (GR732187), where a right turn down the road leads past Herbert's Quarry to the lower car park after 500m.

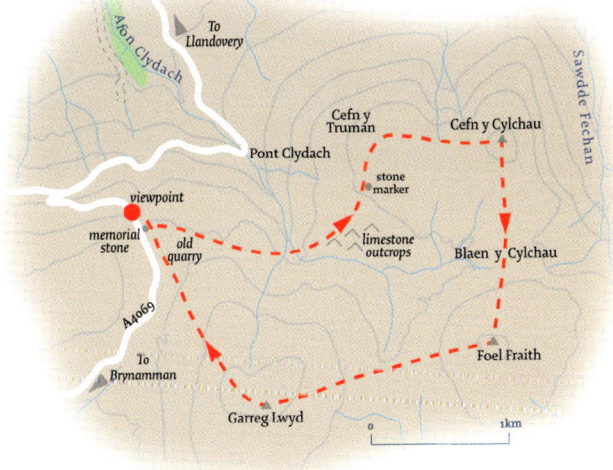

◀ Foel Fraith from Cefn y Truman

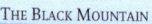

Tair Carn Uchaf

Distance 9km **Time** 3 hours 30
Terrain remote moorland with some pathless sections; total height gain 250m
Map OS Explorer OL12 **Access** no public transport to the start

Pick your way slowly over the rough heather moorland to the three massive cairns which tower above the fairytale Carreg Cennen Castle.

From a distance, this castle has the appearance of every child's imagination, perched as it is on top of an impressive crag with its seemingly impregnable white cliffs. The first defences on the site are said to have been built by the knights of King Arthur – one of them still sleeps beneath the castle, ever ready to rise again when called on to defend the Welsh.

Start from the parking area on the mountain road, 2km west of the A4069 (GR707193). Across the road take the bridleway track which winds its way southwards uphill (after 100m ignore a track bearing left) and in 1km reaches a boggy ford over an area of streams. Continue a little further to just beyond the point where some limestone blocks line the path before the brow of the hill.

Here, bear right off the bridleway and strike out WSW for 2km over the heather moorland on pathless and at times rough terrain, crossing a boggy low point after 800m, before climbing a little towards the three massive cairns on Tair Carn Uchaf (480m) and the reward of some magnificent views. Continue along the hill's broad ridge for another 1.2km to the lower top of Tair Carn Isaf, which has the hill's triangulation point.

From here, descend NNW down grassy slopes with views to Carreg Cennen

◀ Looking north to Carreg Cennen Castle

Castle in the distance beyond a small intervening ridge. The first identifiable fortifications on the site are attributed to Prince Rhys ap Gruffudd in the 12th century and, therefore, notable for being built by someone other than the Normans, though much of what survives now dates from the time of Edward I. The castle was attacked by Owain Glyndwr in 1403, but its demise came 60 years later during the Wars of the Roses, when it was slighted and abandoned to prevent its further use as a Lancastrian stronghold.

Cross the stream at the bottom of the slope and head up the small ridge ahead, making to the left of a prominent old quarry. Once on the crest, turn right and follow the track northeastwards, passing above the quarry. Here, the track gives out, but continue in the same direction along the broadening ridge for 800m to a point where you can descend to a large swallow hole, which is used by cavers to enter a cave system.

Now, still heading in the same direction, cross a flatter area of shake holes and peat hags, keeping to their left, and aim for the point, 1km ahead, where the steeper slopes on the right start to flatten out. Once here, pick up a prominent sheep trod, which soon crosses a stream before becoming a grassy track as it approaches the mountain road. Bear right, where a short pull up the road for 250m will return you to the start.

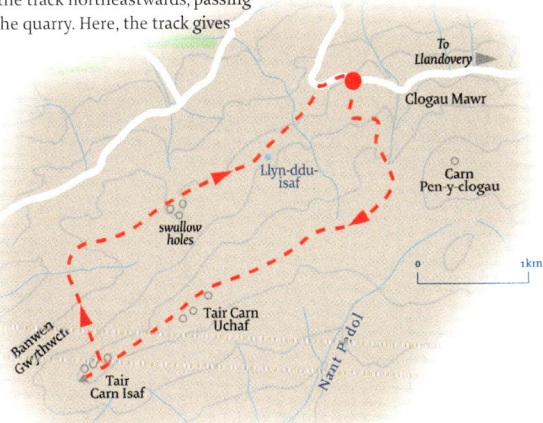

Index

Abergavenny	22
Allt yr Esgair	30
Bannau Brycheiniog	88
Beacons Way	30, 44, 60, 90
Black Darren	10
Black Hill	8
Black Mountain	84, 86, 88, 90, 92, 94
Black Mountains	6, 8, 10, 12, 14, 16, 18, 20, 22, 24, 26, 28, 30
Blaenavon	36
Blorenge, The	34
Brecon	48
Bwlch	30
Carreg Cennen Castle	94
Castell Coch (Red Castle)	80
Chartist Cave	42
Chwarel y Fan	14
Clydach Gorge	38
Corn Du	50, 54, 58
Craig Cerrig-gleisiad	72
Craig y Cilau	40
Cribyn	52, 54, 58
Crug Hywel	26
Cwm Claisfer	42
Cwm Du	70
Cwm Gwdi	50, 54
Cwm Sorgwm	28
Cwmcrawnon	44
Cwmyoy	16
Defynnog	74
Fan Brycheiniog	88, 90
Fan Fawr	72, 80
Fan Frynych	70
Fan Gyhirych	76
Fan Hir	90
Fan Llia	80
Fan Nedd	74, 78
Fan y Big	56
Fforest Fawr	66, 68, 70, 74, 72, 76, 78, 80, 82
Foel Fraith	92
Garreg Lwyd	92
Gilwern	38
Glyntawe	90
Govilon	38
Hatterall Hill	16
Hay Bluff	12
Libanus	68, 70
Llanbedr	26
Llanfoist	34
Llanfrynach	56
Llangattock	40
Llangorse Lake	30
Llangynidr	42
Llanthony	14, 16
Macnamara's Road	25
Maen Llia	78
Monmouthshire & Brecon Canal	34, 38, 40, 44
Mynydd Coety (Coity Mountain)	36
Mynydd Illtud	68, 70
Mynydd Llangorse	28, 30
Mynydd Myddfai	86
Mynydd Troed	28
Neuadd Reservoirs	58
Offa's Dyke Path	10, 12, 16
Pant y Creigiau	62
Pen Allt-mawr	26
Pen Cerrig-calch	26
Pen-y-Crug	48
Pen y Fan	50, 54, 58
Pen y Gadair Fawr	24
Picws Du	88
Pontsticill	62, 64
Pontneddfechan	82
Sarn Helen	70, 74, 78
Senni Valley	74
Skirrid, The	20
Sugar Loaf	22
Taff Trail	60, 64, 72
Tair Carn Uchaf	94
Talybont Reservoir	60
Tor y Foel	44
Twmpa	12
Twyn y Gaer (Libanus)	68
Twyn y Gaer (Llanthony)	18
Usk Reservoir	86
Usk Valley	44
Vale of Ewyas	14
Waun Fach	24
Waun Rydd	60
Ysgyryd Fawr	20
Ystradfellte	78, 80
Ystrad Stone	64